BEN MILLARD

FATHER OF THE BADLANDS,

A GRANDSON'S VIEW

BY

Dr. George Millard

First Edition
Copyright 2019, Dr. George Millard

ISBN 978-0-578-43697-5
Library of Congress Control Number 2018915151
Published by:
      George Millard
      15 Robb Farm Rd
      Saint Paul, MN 55217-2526
      (651) 484-6950
Edited by Scribendi
Cover photo by George Millard.
Email the Author at: george@millardmanor.com

Ben Herbert Millard

"So indeed, it is most fitting that Ben Millard was known far and wide as the 'Father of the Badlands National Monument'."

National Reserve Life Insurance Company: S. H. Witmer, Chairman of the Board of Directors and H. O. Chapman President (Ben Millard was Dean member of the board)

Table of Contents

Introduction 1

SECTION 1: "THE BOOM" – EAST RIVER COUNTRY

Chapter 1: The Early Years 6

Chapter 2: Good Times Abound – Ben's Marriage, No Income Tax, and the Banking Business 17

Chapter 3: Growing a Diverse Business 24

Chapter 4: Ruskin Park 1900–1925 30

SECTION 2: "THE BUST" – EAST RIVER COUNTRY

Chapter 5: Farmland Market Bust and Grasshopper Plagues 53

SECTION 3: "THE BADLANDS EPIC" – WEST RIVER COUNTRY

Chapter 6: Ben Millard Meets the Badlands and Senator Norbeck 65

Chapter 7: Surveying the Road, Cedar Pass, Pinnacles, and My First Visit 81

Chapter 8: The Depression Years –Ben Millard Buys and Donates Land for Badlands National Monument........98

Chapter 9: The World War II Years – Ben and Stella Millard Face Years of Scarcity and Gas Rationing 112

Chapter 10: Life at the Lodge, Inside and Outside, Heralded Out Front by Dewey and Alice Beard's Tepee.....137

Chapter 11: The Progressive View Must Continue! 166

Acknowledgments 176

Bibliography 181

Index 184

Introduction

First Prairie Road Trip to the Badlands, Spring of 1936

Toward the end of 1935, famous architect Frank Lloyd Wright was one of the first national figures to travel the just-completed Badlands National Park Loop Road in South Dakota. Afterward, Wright wrote and published glowing reports of the automobile trip. Jay Shuler cites a few words:

> As we rode, or seemed to be floating, upon a splendid winding road that seemed to understand it all and just where to go [Wright rhapsodized], we rose and fell between its delicate parallels of rose and cream and sublime shapes, chalk white, fretted against a blue sky with high floating clouds—the sky itself seemed only there to cleanse and light the vast harmonious building-scheme. (1989, p. 29)

The road had been surveyed by foot and on horseback by Ben Millard (my grandfather) and US Senator Peter Norbeck of South Dakota. In their minds, the main priority of a new road through the Badlands was to give tourists the best possible views of the spectacular scenery. Getting all the involved public, state, and federal agencies to agree had been a chore. The roadbuilding process presents a vivid historical lesson.[1] It had been no easy task to walk and plot a road, as anyone familiar with the Badlands knows. Just to walk a straight line or plot a straight course through jumbled canyons, crags, and cliffs the size of small mountains required many steep ascents and descents. Working together, these men visualized the different views of the Badlands' expanses as they would be seen from their new road.

Following Grandfather's trek over these many years, I became more and more curious about his history, learning experiences, and developed skills. For example, how did he develop such a professional and commanding speaking ability? Every night, in front of Cedar Pass Lodge in the Badlands, I watched him give thoroughly knowledgeable, well-prepared, and most definitely well-delivered lectures on the Badlands. I also wondered how he learned to build and then manage all the activities, people, and resources necessary to run a place like Cedar Pass Lodge.

The list of his abilities, competencies, and skills unknown to me kept growing. I would often hear names of places in eastern South Dakota. Every now and then, I would hear my father (Glen Millard) or my aunt (Faye Millard MacFarland) talk about Ruskin Park and the 400 or 500 cars driving there. Sometimes, I would get a glimpse of long-forgotten photos as well. Even though my wife Patty and I had lived a year or more in Huron, South Dakota, only forty or so miles north of Ruskin Park, we never went there.

Then, one day, on a drive to the Badlands from Minnesota five or six years ago, I decided to go by way of Artesian, South Dakota because Dad (Glen Millard) often talked about it, and I knew

---

[1] National Park Service objective studies made some eighty years later (e.g., the Historic Resource Study of the Badlands by John Milner Associates, Inc. in 2006) showed how the development of the Badlands National Park should be consulted as a model for future parks or monuments. This observation appears particularly relevant now when the debate at the national level seems hell-bent on opening previously protected areas to various extractive uses.

that he as well as Uncle Herb and Aunt Dorothy were born there. About nine miles west of Artesian, on Highway 34, I was astonished to see the new historic plaque about Ruskin Park. I have to admit, I felt equally stupid and embarrassed!

How could it be that I hadn't seen all the many mentions of my grandfather's involvement in Ruskin Park in newspaper accounts or books written about him, or even in his eulogy in the US Congressional Record? At Grandfather's funeral, he was eulogized as follows:

> [As] "Father of the Badlands" . . . the strength of the man and the breadth of his vision can only be encompassed by the awe-inspiring vistas offered by the region which he loved and developed. Ben Millard passed away amid his beloved surroundings at Cedar Pass Lodge on March 23rd, 1956. (National Reserve Life Insurance Company, 1956)

I attended Grandfather's funeral and also the memorial service. The next year, I witnessed the Millard Ridge Dedication at Cedar Pass Lodge on June 28th, 1957. Still, I heard very little about Ruskin Park—I must have been living in some sort of a cocoon with earmuffs on.

My own life has been very full and satisfying. I grew up filling my heart and soul with the Badlands. The first family trip to the Badlands in 1936 hooked me. During summer breaks in the 1940s, I spent weeks working at the lodge. In the 1950s, I was an educated young adult and newly married. When I introduced my wife, Patty, to the Badlands, she fell in love with the place and the people. The 1950s were educational because Grandfather's passing in 1956 energized me to learn as much as possible about him and his passion—the Badlands. In 1963, Cedar Pass Lodge was sold.

After 1972, I interviewed my aging family members and old friends in South Dakota about the Badlands, Ruskin Park, and Grandfather Millard. I've also enjoyed a close relationship with the Institute of Historical Survey Foundation (IHSF), which assisted me in my research. In addition, I spoke often with members of the Badlands Natural History Association. To both of these groups, I donated family artifacts and shared important documents.

In 2018, I wrote a book about our Peace Corps experiences—*The Peace Corps, A Family's Response to JFK's Call: Accept the Challenge*—which had me sifting through a large cache of information. I encountered my collection of notes and original source materials on the Badlands and my grandfather, Ben Millard. I was energized and driven to write by the dramatic changes in the US political scene of 2016. It seemed we, as a people, were turning our backs on two important American civic responsibilities: (1) positive international engagement using such groups as the Peace Corps, and, (2) conserving our sacred natural wonders here at home.

My grandfather and Senator Norbeck were philosophically cut from the same cloth. They both followed the ideals of the Progressive movement. Norbeck's involvement in progressivism is well documented:

> Norbeck was a pioneer in the Progressive Movement during the early 1900s, and he advanced the idea of being progressive in trying to improve American society, economic inequalities and cleaning up political corruption. . . . Norbeck was unique in looking at how to provide for the best interests of the American public, not a particular group . . . He did not oppose capitalism, but rather unreasonable profit. A progressive Republican in a rural state wasn't exactly a common theme in the early 20th century, but Norbeck

was one of four [governors] during that period of time to be considered a progressive

Republican. (Fosness, 2018)

In 1975, Dennis J. Hall popularized a statement of unknown origin on conservation that I have held dear ever since:

"We have not inherited the land from our fathers; we have borrowed it from our children." (n.d.)

SECTION 1: "THE BOOM" – EAST RIVER COUNTRY

Chapter 1: The Early Years

Ben Millard's work career began as a midwestern farm boy born in Lake Crystal in Blue Earth County of southern Minnesota. He was born on September 15th, 1872, seven years after the end of the US Civil War. Ben's earliest years were documented in this memorial tribute:

> His boyhood was typical, being spent largely on the farm where he was born. About 1880, his parents [Riley Milton Millard and Mary (Francis) Hull] moved to Lyons, Nebraska, where they established farm operations. Later, the Millard family moved into the area of Pender, Nebraska.
>
> At the age of 14, Ben Millard started working on a ferryboat which operated on the Missouri River, from Decatur, Nebraska and later worked as a cow hand on one of the large cattle ranches in the region. (National Reserve Life Insurance Company, 1956)

Decatur is described in various accounts as having a long and colorful history. Interestingly, Lyons, Nebraska, where the Millard family first moved from Minnesota when young Ben was about eight years old, was much later combined with Decatur. As a result, he would have become familiar with Decatur as a young boy because the two towns were either contiguous or at least in very close proximity.

In 1886, it is likely that Ben still lived on the family farm. Presumably, his father and mother were still operating the farm as both were still in their thirties.

Adding to its colorful background is the fact that Decatur combines a principal landmark with a geographical and historical feature of the town. According to the "History of Decatur, Nebraska," as written in *A History of Burt County from 1903 to 1929,*

> During the summer of 1819, Lewis and Clark came up the Missouri River from Ft. Calhoun and visited the grave of Chief Blackbird. The site is about 8 or 9 miles north of the original townsite of Decatur. Here they planted a small American flag. At this time, the grave of the famous chief, about whom so many stories are told, was marked by a great mound of earth some 45 feet in height and 30 feet in circumference. For as many as 35 years, no sign of the huge mound has been seen by those who visit the grave. The chief died in 1800 and on his deathbed asked that he be buried on the highest hill overlooking the Missouri, and despite a century and a quarter of exposure to the elements, it still has that distinction. Much has been written about the chief, but all agree his influence over his people was great and that he used this influence to make peace between the red men and the pale face. His dying message to people was much like this, "The white man is our friend; therefore, let my spirit rest in peace on the highest hill of the Missouri, so that as they pass up and down, I may see them and welcome them to my children and my land of beautiful forests and prairies and plenty."

> Tradition tells us Blackbird learned in some way the use of strychnine and used this knowledge in a strange way. Occasionally he would announce at every tent that a

certain brave was soon to die or had been called by the spirit God, the doomed man always did die and so the story runs, no one but Blackbird [also known as] Wa-kar-me, the medicine man, knew the real cause, so this might account for obedience accorded Blackbird, but not for the love his people had for him nor for the dying wish for peace with the white man. (1929, p. 1)

This story of Decatur and Chief Blackbird might seem to be an interesting diversion from my grandfather's story, but some details and connections come up later in my grandfather's journey that relate to these early influences on him. First, white settlers living with or in close proximity to Native American villages or encampments was a way of life. Second, as a boy, Ben was exposed to these legends. He likely visited Chief Blackbird's grave more than once with friends over the years, until he was eighteen years old when he left to go to Shenandoah Normal College. He certainly knew some Native American languages and later spoke some Lakota when he lived in the Badlands.

This part of his life experience is important for later events as another connecting of trails with a second famous Native American, Dewey Beard, takes place somewhere in the early Badlands days. They may have met even earlier because many members of the Pine Ridge Native American Reservation were employed at Cedar Pass Lodge over the years.

A bit more on Decatur paints a picture of the times and town that Ben knew. Decatur, one of Nebraska's earliest river towns on the Missouri River, is where Ben began to work on ferryboats, which carried wagons and cars across the river well into the 1930s. The following are lively descriptions of Decatur in the late 1800s:

Decatur, second oldest settlement in Nebraska, is rich in Indian legend, tales of explorers, and pioneers. Among the first white men in this area were those from the Lewis & Clark Expedition while on their exploration of the newly acquired territory in 1804. . . . A railroad company, organized in Decatur in 1857, resulted in the first railroad survey from the west bank of the Missouri River. . . . Located at the foot of a high bluff, the fortunes of Decatur are closely tied to the Missouri River. During the heyday of river traffic many boats tied up at the Decatur landing, bringing supplies, lumber, and people. Ferryboats carried horses, wagons, and cars across the river until 1930s. In the meantime the fickle Missouri, after one of its rampages, shifted its channel to the east leaving the bridge high and dry. (Maryott, 2005)

Prairie fires were not uncommon in the early days and many times the cemetery has been swept by one and the villagers terrorized. . . . There were several Indian scares and once word came down from the north that the Sioux were on the warpath and intended coming on to the settlement at Decatur. This time many became so frightened that they left their homes and land and fled only to return in a few days when the rumor was proven false. (History of Decatur, Nebraska, 1929, p. 5)

From 1869 to 1880, the population of Decatur fell, so when Ben started working in 1884, Decatur was called a village. I'm not sure when it was declared a city once more, but the first newspaper, the *Decatur Herald,* was printed in 1881. In any case, Decatur was certainly a frontier town. With no bridge, ferries and boats were the only ways to cross the Missouri river.

Decatur was a somewhat primitive and isolated town. In those days, people got around on riverboats, horses, and horse-drawn carriages, so Ben started out in kind of a pioneer area. There must have been stories at least in Decatur newspapers or magazines of Indian uprisings because the Battle of the Little Big Horn took place when Ben was four years old in 1876. In 1891, when Ben was a sophomore at Shenandoah Normal College, Dewey Beard, the Sioux Indian chief was wounded and several of his family members killed at the Massacre at Wounded Knee. Dewey Beard was born in 1862 and died in 1955.

Along with reports and articles in the media of the day regarding Indian uprisings, these events were certainly communicated in person by land or river travelers and later by railroad travelers. One more observation from "History of Decatur, Nebraska" concerning Indians and early settlers is particularly graphic. The following quote cements the concept that the area around Decatur could certainly be looked at as a part of the Wild West:

> The Missouri River has perhaps played the largest single role in Decatur's history. It was the means of the first settlers getting here. It formed a distinct boundary line on one side of which the early settlers were safe from Indians, but when they crossed the river they need not be surprised if they were raided, scalped and left to die on the prairie by warring Omahas or Sioux. (1929, pp. 6-7)

The railroad lines kept multiplying into the West in Ben's youth. As mentioned earlier, Ben and his family had moved to Lyons in about 1880. It may have been a big family event to watch the final stages of the Omaha & Northern Nebraska Railway arriving in Lyons. Young Ben probably spent some time near the railroad. The arrival and departure of the trains would have been important occurrences in the town.

Railroads had quite an effect and made an impression on my dad and his sister, Faye . My father often talked about how the railroad conductor was considered a significant and important figure in South Dakota communities. Most of the time, my dad wore a three-piece suit, and he always carried a conductor's watch with a gold-colored chain attached in the vest pocket. To tell the time, he would ceremoniously take out the watch, push the button, and flip open the front, explaining, "The time is, (such and such)." Then, with practiced accuracy, he would drop the watch back into his vest pocket. Although he may have had wristwatches later in life, I can't recall anything but the vivid scene of his pocket watch. By the same token, I'm also fixated on many railroad stories, sights, and sounds, and I recollect the sounds of the old steam engines, climbing the long hill from downtown St. Paul, westward to Minneapolis. I heard it every night for years after I'd gone to bed. It always refreshed my mind before I went to sleep.

Aunt Faye Millard MacFarland also used to tell me about their railroad trips back from California to South Dakota. Chapter 4, "Ruskin Park 1900–1925," includes a description of her railroad experiences and those of my father and myself. Railroads, along with post offices, in small rural towns were so important that the arrival and departure of trains, especially passenger or combination passenger and freight trains, was a social, business, and often festive event where townspeople could see friends, hear the news, pass on information, and more.

A good example from back in the 1940s comes to mind. I spent parts of those summers in the Badlands and at Cedar Pass Lodge, and there were many trips to the train depot in the town of Interior, South Dakota. One train a day came through for Rapid City, South Dakota, and everyone knew when it would arrive. We hardly missed a day going to the depot for freight. Grandfather , of course, never missed a day during the season because he had to take his packet of cash in a thick, registered-mail envelope to the post office to send it off with the daily receipts to the bank in Rapid City. Driving that route by car would have been a daily 200-mile round trip to the bank in "Rapid" (as they called Rapid City). Such a trip would have been impossible during the height of the tourist season when every family member was needed for regular tasks. Grandfather couldn't waste the travel time as he was absolutely necessary for appearances or short lectures in the dining room or to talk to distinguished guests and visitors at the lodge.

So, as 1890 approached, Ben's trek took a turn. He had been thinking about continuing his education. The move from the family farm to college was the catalyst for more big changes in Ben's life. At the college in Shenandoah that year, a freak event necessitated a move the next year to Lincoln, Nebraska. The move to Lincoln is notable because it sets the stage for a meeting with a prominent local banker, W. A. Loveland, with interests stretching into South Dakota . Perhaps it was just a coincidence, as we all know luck plays a big part in career tracks, but these events do seem to pile up both early and late along Ben's career. I've always believed, based on what I saw and heard over the years, that Grandfather was the right man, in the right place, and at exactly the right time, to end up later as the "Father of the Badlands."

Ben chose an interesting college to attend in 1890. In Shenandoah, a huge change occurred in 1884 in the college ownership and administration when Professor Croan came to town. He had previously been superintendent of schools in Madison County, Indiana, and he enjoyed a sterling career as an educator. About Croan, it was reported:

> He was editor and proprietor of the *Anderson Democrat* for five years. . . Prof. Croan resigned the office of county superintendent in the early spring of 1884, and moved to Shenandoah, Iowa, where he had just purchased the entire property of the Western Normal College. When he took possession, he found only sixty-five students. The name and fame of the school advanced from that time. The *Iowa Normal Monthly* says: "Prof. Croan accomplished a work at Shenandoah which not one man in a thousand would have done." The enrollment the last year there [1891] was something more than forty-three hundred. (JNO Lethem, 1892, p. 247)

In seven years, Professor Croan increased student enrollment from 65 students to 4,235 when he bought and took over the college. That amazing figure reflects an average of ten times the student population per year using the starting figure. And, of course, because Professor Croan had to crank out his marketing, courses, and so on at the beginning, he would have been unlikely to hit that figure in the first year. Word must have spread around a wide area, and the attraction certainly must have caught Ben's attention at some point. Although Shenandoah is about 120 miles from Decatur, Nebraska, it's reasonable to conclude that news of what was going on at that college would have reached Lyons and Decatur.

What happened next at the college directly affected Ben's way, according to historical reports:

On the night of December 2, 1891, a dire calamity came upon the Western Normal College. Fire, in its fury, took possession of the entire structure and routed students, faculty, proprietor and president. Apparently, the destruction was total, but a second thought reminded us that only the hull was gone, while the kernel containing the germ of life, was secure. The best part of the college was in the minds and hearts of its thousands of students and the inhabitants of this western country. . . . Prof. Croan had magnificent offers from forty-seven different cities to relocate the college with them. Lincoln was finally chosen as the place best suited for the work of the school on account of its railroad facilities, geographical location, capital of a great state, educational center of the West. . . . The bonus given Prof. Croan at Lincoln is the largest ever given in the United States, This at once shows the value placed upon his rare executive ability. (JNO Lethem, 1892, p. 248)

It doesn't take much imagination to appreciate why a beginning college student, enthusiastic and determined to improve his education as Ben continued to be all his life, would have accepted the challenge and moved to Lincoln to attend the newly named Western Normal College. Likely, Professor Croan must have either directly or indirectly influenced Ben and other students, considering what the professor, his college, administrators, faculty staff, and students had gone through and come out of so well.

So, 1891 saw Ben joining his classmates in the move to Lincoln. At nineteen years old, he was in his sophomore year, which is typical in many colleges. This year also marked Ben's first entry into the banking business.

He was given the opportunity to begin work in the Lesterville, South Dakota, State Bank

by Mr. W. A. Loveland, prominent banker of the time in South Dakota and Nebraska.

Young Millard worked in this bank for a period of several years. (National Reserve Life

Insurance Company, 1956)

Where and when Ben first met Loveland isn't clear. However, Ben's move to the Western

Normal College in Lincoln appears to have been the catalyst in beginning the business

relationship with W. A. Loveland. Lesterville, South Dakota, which is located on the Missouri

River, is around 240 miles from Lincoln. Ben enjoyed river towns, so the move was easy, and

with his college studies on hold, he started working in the banking business.

All the river towns he lived in and all the rivers he traveled on had long-lasting influences on

young Ben. He was very familiar with river vacationers, the potential for tourism on a daily

basis, short vacations, and longer visits during hot summer months. For example, his most

significant and largest ventures in real estate and multiuse family, amusement, sporting, and

racing parks took place on the James River. All of Chapter 4 later in this book is devoted to the

development of Ruskin Park as it was the foundation of a large percentage of his personal

lifetime fortune—all as a result of his efforts in this southeastern portion of South Dakota

during the heyday of good times during the 1890s–1910s. Ruskin Park was located right on the

James River only some forty-five miles west of Sioux Falls, South Dakota. Its suburb, Canton,

South Dakota, would turn out to be the next major waypoint on his road to the Badlands.

In any case, it's fascinating how these coincidences lined up for Grandfather. He decided to

enroll in Shenandoah just as the student body numbers were exploding, and then the whole school burned down, causing him to relocate to Lincoln. The move to Lincoln leds him not only

to meet Loveland, who offered him a position in his bank, but also to meet his future wife,

Stella Neely.

Chapter 2: Good Times Abound – Ben's Marriage, No Income Tax, and the Banking Business

In 1894, Ben chose to enter the feedstore business in Canton, South Dakota (National Reserve Life Insurance Company, 1956), which was a good fit given his extensive background with cattle and agriculture. Plus, the location of Canton, South Dakota, which is only twenty miles from Sioux Falls, worked out perfectly because Sioux Falls is by far South Dakota's largest, most populous, and biggest dollar-producing city in the state.

To understand and appreciate Ben's successes in his new venture in 1894, a somewhat more detailed look at the highly unusual tax and economic conditions of the times is critical. It's useful, educational, and interesting to review what was happening on a national scale.

First, in that decade and beyond, there was no federal income tax! No federal income tax at all seems unimaginable now. Only a small number of historians recall what took place 140 to 150 years ago in 1872, the year Ben was born. The taxation story was such a major event that it's essential to an understanding of how a farm boy, now twenty-two, could begin to amass a small fortune starting from close to nothing.

One thing to know is that Ben, as the story shows, was exceptionally careful with his money and expenses. He worked night and day and maintained very good credit as was attested to in a eulogy by a prominent South Dakota banker at my grandfather's funeral services. Ben was no fly-by-night, impulsive type of businessman; however, he was definitely willing to "bet the farm" on some venture if he was convinced it was a good investment after reviewing all the details. During these times in the 1890s, those convictions paid off handsomely.

At the dedication of Millard Ridge at the Badlands National Monument in 1957, the year after Ben's death, the president of the Black Hills National Bank, Robert E. Driscoll, gave the following eulogy for my grandfather:

> Looking back through history is difficult, but necessary to obtain a proper perspective. I always look forward to Mrs. Millard and Ben coming to Rapid City and into our bank. It was always a social gathering, followed by whatever business they had in mind. . . . Sometimes they needed money, but many times they did not. If they needed financing, they got it because their credit was their religion which they guarded carefully and seriously. This care and zeal has been transmitted to their family, to Herbert [Grandfather's youngest son] who is running the family business. . . . Therefore I feel honored to say a word of eulogy to this great man and participate, also as humbly as he would in this dedication. (National Reserve Life Insurance Company, 1956)

The extended tax holiday of the 1890s was so unusual that a quick reminder of what and when it happened is not only enlightening but also a striking coincidence, along with others later on in Ben's life. You might even begin to believe that the repeal of the income tax in 1872 was a birthday gift to my grandfather to start off his life.

Several online accounts agree with Wikipedia's assessment of the various revenue changes at the time:

In order to help pay for its war effort in the American Civil War, Congress imposed its first personal income tax in 1861. . . . Congress also enacted the Revenue Act of 1862, which levied a 3% tax on incomes above $600, rising to 5% for incomes above $10,000. Rates were raised in 1864. This income tax was repealed in 1872. (History of Taxation in The United States, n.d., p. 3)[2]

Then, another major event occurred in 1894 and 1895, just as Ben had entered the feedstore business in Canton, after having spent several years in the Lesterville, South Dakota, bank business. It is well known that in the earliest years of our country—and still today in less-developed countries—tariffs were a proven method for collecting taxes efficiently, fairly, and without huge costs.

Tariffs have played different parts in trade policy and the economic history of the United States. Tariffs were the largest source of federal revenue from the 1790s to the eve of World War I, until it was surpassed by income taxes. Since the revenue from the tariff was considered essential and easy to collect at the major ports, it was agreed the nation should have a tariff for revenue purposes.

Another role the tariff played was in the protection of local industry. . . . A new income tax statute was enacted as part of the 1894 Tariff Act. At that time, the United States Constitution specified that Congress could impose a "direct" tax only if the law apportioned that tax among the states according to each state's census population. (History of Taxation in The United States, n.d., p. 3)

---

[2] n.d. is required in the APA format style of referencing quotes to indicate no publishing date for the information cited.

However, this action by Congress caused a snarl with the Supreme Court and in effect gave another gift of a long tax extension relief to those occupied—as Ben was—in agriculture, real estate, interest income, and other income from personal property. The case at the court was as follows:

In 1895, the United States Supreme Court ruled, in *Pollock v. Farmers' Loan & Trust Co.*, that taxes on rents from real estate, on interest income from personal property and other income from personal property (which includes dividend income) were direct taxes on property and therefore had to be apportioned. Since apportionment of income taxes is impractical, the *Pollock* rulings had the effect of prohibiting a federal tax on income from property. Due to the political difficulties of taxing individual wages without taxing income from property, a federal income tax was impractical from the time of the *Pollock* decision until the time of ratification of the Sixteenth Amendment. (History of Taxation in The United States, n.d., p. 6)

These two events paved the way right down the center of the alley of Ben's interests and eliminated any income tax all the way to 1913 when the Sixteenth Amendment to the Constitution was proposed. Ben would benefit from this second gift of no income tax from age twenty-four to forty-one, when the law changed back to allow income tax collection.

Even better, although the federal income tax was reimposed when a sufficient number of states ratified the Sixteenth Amendment to the Constitution, it was still quite possible for successful business, agriculture, and real estate people to accumulate funds from their activities for at least five more years.

In 1918, as the United States was raising money to pay for military expenses in World War I, the rates jumped way up (relative to what the situation had been since 1872) for high-income earners:

> Congress enacted an income tax in October 1913 as part of the Revenue Act of 1913, levying a 1% tax on net personal incomes above $3,000, with a 6% surtax on incomes above $500,000. By 1918, the top rate of the income tax was increased to 77% (on income over $1,000,000, equivalent of $16,717,815 in 2018 dollars to finance World War I). The average rate for the rich however, was 15%. (History of Taxation in The United States, n.d., pp. 6–7)

Such good luck with favorable exogenous variables from Ben's point of view was going to change down the line, but his habits were established, and personal resilience would once again carry he and his wife Stella through some shockingly unusual times and events down the trail.

Speaking of his wife, it was the next year, in 1896, when Grandfather made one of his best decisions as far as he and the rest of our family is concerned when he married Stella Neely, with whom he had become acquainted while both of them were college students in Lincoln, Nebraska. They were married on May 20, 1896.

Five Generation Photo

Taken in 1902. (*left to right*) Great grandfather Rufus Merritt (67), mother Estella Neely Millard (27), Glen Millard (father of author) (5), grandmother Mary Wiles Neely (44), great-great grandmother Edna Combs Merritt (95)

One additional paragraph is appropriate to mention here from the memorial tribute presented to family and guests at Grandfather's memorial services in 1956. The sixty-year passage of time from their wedding until his death allowed the senior officers of the National Reserve Life Insurance company to follow his journey and observe the consistent characteristics of his life:

It is interesting to note [how] this young couple started their marriage life. Through a program of rigid and consistent savings, they managed to accumulate enough to buy a lot, and the young husband, by working at night, built their first home. The couple's first child, Glen E. Millard, was born while residing in this house in Canton, S.D., in 1897. A year later, Ben Millard, through the interest of his friend, Mr. W. A. Loveland was again offered an opportunity—this time that of operating the Artesian State Bank in Artesian, South Dakota. Selling his interest in the feed store, young Millard went immediately to take up his banking duties at Artesian. Within about another year, his friend, Mr. W. A.

22

Loveland, decided to relinquish some of his own bank holdings, and in turn Millard was given the opportunity to purchase the Artesian State Bank. It took all Ben Millard's ability to raise all of the necessary capital but he did manage to do so and entered upon this phase of his colorful career. (National Reserve Life Insurance Company, 1956)

Chapter 3: Growing a Diverse Business

Ben's steaming hot business and development career hit its peak performance rate when he was twenty-six years old in 1898. That was the year in which W. A. Loveland offered him the opportunity to manage the Artesian State Bank. In that position, Ben would have come in contact with a number and variety of customers, potential customers, and organizations related to the town government and local happenings and plans.

One of those people, in particular, was Robert Emmett Dowdell with whom he later purchased Ruskin Park and hundreds of acres of land along the James River. Between the two of them, in what was a town of only a few square blocks, they had become the top businessmen. Dowdell, whose very substantial and energetic background likened him to Ben, was the owner and publisher of the *Sanborn County Advocate* newspaper. In addition, he and his wife ran the Arlington Hotel,[3] and about the time that Ben entered the feedstore business in Canton, Dowdell became a member of the South Dakota House of Representatives in Pierre, South Dakota. He held the seat for two years. Dowdell then served as a member of the South Dakota Senate. He was elected to that seat for a total of four noncontiguous terms from 1907 to 1932.

Dowdell was Ben's senior by fifteen years, and their combined sources of information about what was happening locally, and also what plans were in the winds for the future, were bound

---

[3] A more detailed description of Dowdell's activities is also footnoted in the next chapter: *Artesian, South Dakota Centennial History 1883–1983,* published in 1982, p. 132.

to be high level and reliable. Therefore, between the two of them, they would certainly have been aware of the extent and trend of the operations at nearby Ruskin Park. The park was located on Highway 34 only eight miles to the west of Artesian, and two-and-a-half miles from the next town of Forestburg, South Dakota.

On a personal note, to manage all these life-changing stages in a young couple's adventures, Grandfather and Grandmother, as I saw many times in later life, worked well together as a family unit. As we know, one doesn't just build the outside of a house. Furniture, shelving, and so on are all a part of the process. A lot of decision making and critical thinking is required. It takes a knowledgeable mother to ensure there is designated storage space for clean vs dirty baby laundry, supplies, food, etc. As the homemaker, Grandmother must have been very involved at the same time caring for baby Glen.

The lives of Grandfather and Grandmother were on a whirlwind course in very good times in the early and mid-1990s. But, later on, there were times that put all of them close to their wits' ends as outside forces bore down on them with bad tidings.

As an example of continuing the family enterprise, the Millards were an acting ensemble, participating together in Ruskin Park activities. For example, my father was director of, and actor in, some of the Ruskin Park plays where Grandfather also acted as one of the main characters. The newspaper write-ups of the plays were very favorable for all the family actors, the director, and the stage settings. Even after they had moved to California, summer after summer they kept coming back to put on performances and enjoy life at Ruskin Park. In addition to all that:

As time passed, Millard added to his banking interests and organized two new banks, one in Fedora [SD] and the other in Forestburg, South Dakota. His reputation for fair dealing, honesty and hard work brought consistent reward and culminated in the result of Millard further being able to expand his interests through the acquiral of farm property in the area. (National Reserve Life Insurance Company, 1956)

He also began considering buying more real estate in the immediate or nearby areas.

In 1917, disposing of some of his bank holdings, Mr. Millard became actively engaged in real estate, and 2 years later moved to Huron, South Dakota, to become a senior partner of a large farm real estate firm [Millard-Keys-Haskell]. His boundless energy and interests knew no limit, and a year later, in 1920 he became interested in the automobile business and established the Huron Auto Supply Company, wholesaling automotive parts and supplies. (National Reserve Life Insurance Company, 1956)

From reading various accounts of Ruskin Park and its real estate holdings (which was jointly owned by Ben and Dowdell), it's not entirely clear how the actual ownership of the real estate was divided up. The accounts differ, but the following is written about Dowdell:

In 1900 R. E. [Dowdell] created an addition in Artesian east['s] two churches then in existence. His growing-up family required more space, so he built a new home in that area. His real estate venture required more time, so he sold the paper [the *Sanborn County Advocate*, which he had purchased in 1892]. . . . It had proved a rewarding enterprise, for he was made president of the South Dakota Press Association. That entitled him to the National Press Association and he was made its president in 1912. He was later inducted into Brookings College Hall of Fame in the field of journalism.

As Mr. Dowdell became more interested and involved in his real estate ventures, in 1910 he induced Mr. Ben Millard, Artesian banker, to become his partner in the purchase of Ruskin Park, which H. A. Rodee had operated as a Chautauqua Grounds, and had given it its name in honor of John Ruskin, poet and essayist of his day. (Centennial Historical Committee, 1982, p. 132)

Forestburg rancher, Ben Zoss, and his wife, Helen, are the current owners of the former Ruskin Park land. He is continually researching the ownerships and sales of portions of the land and has been going through documents at the county clerk's office to find out who owned which lands that changed hands when the 1919 land bust hit.

Zoss is convinced that Ben was shown as the owner of five miles of land on either side of the James River. The partnership between Dowdell and Ben may have specified that, as part of their agreement, it was to be a joint ownership, though the land was registered in Ben's name. Whatever the case, the parcels of land owned for five miles on either side of the James River amounted to a sizable number of acres. And, as shown in Section 2, large parcels of land along the river reverted back to the state for lack of payment of taxes in 1919–1927.

In 1917, when Ben became senior partner in the real estate firm of Millard-Kyes-Haskell with offices in Aberdeen, South Dakota, the ominous clouds of the bottom falling out of the agricultural land market had not yet appeared. In research, I could not find hard evidence that it started to hit Ben until 1919, when it became thoroughly apparent that the boom times had switched to bust times.

Even at that, Ben's exogenous financial situation was quite favorable for income generation until 1919, when a very serious change hit. His participation in all the diverse aspects of the Ruskin Park development, as far as he was concerned, took place in the years 1905–1910.

Beyond those years, however, he became engaged in other ventures and, in many ways, did not divorce himself or his family from Ruskin Park later in life, even though the family had retired to California, as explained in his eulogy:

> Following the elapse of some years and around 1910, Ben Millard considered the possibility of establishing his home in California. Such a move would necessitate closing out all of his interests in South Dakota. Although he spent several winter seasons in California, his heart remained always with South Dakota and so a complete change was never made. (National Reserve Life Insurance Company, 1956)

From much time and many conversation with his daughter (my Aunt Faye of Chicago) at Cedar Pass Lodge, I do know that the family came back in the summers for several years. Another piece of personal information that came from family discussions, which I haven't seen written elsewhere, is that there was a serious disagreement between Grandfather and A. M. Haskell in their real estate firm when Grandfather was in California yet remained active in the real estate decisions. The poor communications then complicated a very substantial investment, which resulted in huge losses.

This discussion of Grandfather building and growing a diverse business does not have a clear-cut ending until he began to consider buying land in the Badlands from his sister, Clara Jennings. At that point, he was also engaged in remodeling existing cabins at the Cedar Pass Lodge area. Those events received serious consideration in the mid-1920s and, specifically, in the spring of 1926, when he first became acquainted with the Badlands. Grandfather seems to have become so enamored with the Badlands that he immediately focused his full attention on any Badlands-related projects that crossed his path.

Chapter 4: Ruskin Park 1900–1925

Ruskin Park was called the "Playground of the Prairie" for good reason. In its heyday, thousands of people driving hundreds of cars visited the site frequently. Now, all that remains is ranch land, a nice historical marker, and the Ruskin Park racetrack, which is only visible from the air.

The children of Walter and Dagmar Siegenthaler owners of the park in the 1950s and 1960s, are pictured with the current owners of the park site, Ben and Helen Zoss. *Left to right*: Karen (Siegenthaler) Crisco, Richard Siegenthaler, and Helen Zoss, Ben Zoss (Admin, 2013).

The South Dakota State Historical Society Markers listing of historical markers records marker #218 (called the Ruskin Park Marker) as "Ruskin Park 1/2 mile south, erected 1957, Sanborn County, Highway 34, just east of the James River."[4]

---

[4] The original marker listing in the SD listing found online refers to the original 1957 marker.

Thanks to the efforts of Joe Tlustos, formerly of SD Public Radio, and Vic Zimmerman, both previous residents of Forestburg, South Dakota, and many contributors (approximately sixty), a new historic metal marker (replacing the lost original) now graces the former entrance road to the park on Highway 34.[5]

As mentioned in the previous chapter, rancher Ben Zoss and his wife, Helen, currently own the site. Ben Zoss, with whom I spent three full days and many years of phone calls recording facts and reports about Ruskin Park and Grandfather's participation in the park, was more than generous with his time as was Helen. He is an avid historian and intimately knows the local geography. He gave me and my companion, attorney Richard Varco,[6] tours of the property, pointing out the old wagon trails, which are clearly still visible, as they were cut into the prairie by continuous traffic from wagon trains. Three or four different well-used sets of tracks were used by wagons heading toward different specific locations. He also pointed out homestead sites and significant park details. For several years, the Zoss's ran a substantial pheasant hunting operation at his lodge on the former Ruskin Park property. During that time, they answered innumerable questions by his interested out-of-state hunting groups by checking records or visiting libraries and county offices. Ben Zoss does not accept statements or speculations easily unless they also fit his observation of, "that is or isn't logical, because . . ."

---

[5] Colored photos of all these mentioned pictures are easily found with a Google search for "Ruskin Park."

[6] Richard Varco was a senior staff member of the Minnesota Attorney General's Office for thirty years and is also a history buff. He agreed to accompany me to audio record discussions with Ben Zoss.

Helen & Ben Zoss

Before Ruskin Park was Ruskin Park regional recreation center, it was called the Ruskin Park Chautauqua Grounds. Hiram A. Rodee owned 2,000 acres of land on the James River. When Hiram's son wanted to attend college, the trip to New York changed the land, as described in the *Sanborn Weekly Journal*:

> Rodee sent his son, Hiram Augustus "Gus" Rodee, Jr. back east to New York in the late 1890s: While he was in the town of Chautauqua, N.Y., Gus became inspired to bring Chautauqua back with him to the natural beauty his father had found on the Jim [James River].

> Chautauqua was an adult education movement started in Chautauqua, N.Y.in the late 1800s. The idea was to bring speakers, performers, musicians, preachers, etc. to communities that otherwise would have little opportunity for entertainment and culture.

> Chautauqua filled a void in the lives of rural Americans well before the information highway was built. The movement caught on, spread throughout the

country and remained popular until the 1920s. . . . The Railway Co. cooperated with Gus's plan by offering special excursion rates to Ruskin Park. The railroad allowed him to build a depot located at the entrance of the park and carriages met the train to bring visitors into the park for 10 cents each way. The first Chautauqua held in Sanborn County was July 2, 3 and 4, 1904, at Ruskin Park. The program had something for everyone, with music from the State World's Fair Band, an address by former U.S. Senator Richard F Pettigrew, a Woonsocket versus Artesian basketball game, more music, addresses and orations. The cost was 15 cents for kids and 25 cents for adults or season passes were sold for 25 and 50 cents. The 1904 season saw another big event with the harvest picnic on Aug. 17. The all-day event boasted music entertainment and a baseball game between Woonsocket and Artesian.

The next years Ruskin Park would host a Chautauqua and Harvest Festival each year, a Sanborn County Democratic Rally and Old Settler's Picnic. The Park gained regular telephone service and fresh groceries were delivered daily. (Admin, 2013, p. 4)

The Rodee family's great spot on the James River attracted a constant stream of campers and weekend revelers. In 1909, the property was sold due to an illness in the Rodee family. The *Sanborn Weekly Journal* again adds great detail:

One of the people who had bought a plot and built a summer home was "Sanborn County Advocate" editor Robert Dowdell. He and Ben H. Millard, owner of the Artesian State Bank, then purchased the entire Rodee Ranch. They divided the ranch into smaller plots and sold them off, providing [their company] working capital to further develop

Ruskin Park. . . . Dowdell and Millard also added a theater, 40 cabins for rentals and improved the racetrack so it could be used for auto races as well as horse races. A ballpark was also put in the middle of the racetrack.

1910 was the first season under the new ownership and through the teens, the Park became the place to go for entertainment in Sanborn County. Picnics, baseball games, speakers, bands, concerts, races and water sports were among the events and entertainment provided under Dowdell and Millard's tenure. (Admin, 2013, p. 5)

Ruskin Park auto race hand bill, 1920s

It was reported in various places that a minimum of 500 and a maximum of 4,700 cars frequented the park on any given summer day. The park was a huge draw in the first part of the 1900s. About 15,000 people a day arrived at Ruskin Park in automobiles, horse-drawn buggies, and special railroad cars (there was a small railroad depot on the north side of the road at that point).

Although Ben was co-owner of the park with Dowdell, Ben was the day-to-day manager and marketing agent according to rancher Ben Zoss. Dowdell was frequently out of town attending meetings as he was a member of the South Dakota State Legislature for many years. Dowdell and Ben greatly increased the variety of entertainment and activities—specifically, they turned Ruskin Park into a music and dance destination by hiring a number of well-known bands to play; the crowds increased dramatically.

As noted in various newspaper articles, Ben was a master at marketing and designing displays. He and Dowdell were privy to information on the possibility of obtaining sections of a huge display from the Louisiana Purchase Exposition in St. Louis, Missouri, which had run in 1904. They bought and brought back two large doors for the dance hall and auditorium. Although it was a giant undertaking, I'm not surprised he did it. Throughout his career, when my grandfather saw something or came up with a plan that he felt would vastly improve the project he was working on, he would not hesitate to go for it. The cost of acquiring, disassembling, and transporting the doors to Ruskin Park must have been one of his biggest gambles, but it became one of his biggest successes as it transformed Ruskin Park. The dance pavilion now had prism glass walls that rose forty feet to the apex, and the maple wood dance floor was lit by gas.

In conversations with Ben Zoss today, he suggested that Grandfather must have arranged for the forty-foot-tall glass doors from the exposition in 1904 to have been boxed or packed somehow and stabilized in a railroad car (presumably covered). Loading and unloading was a substantial job as well as packing and stabilizing the glass doors. Ben Zoss suggested that they likely used double horse-drawn wagons of some sort to get the doors to the park and then reassembled them on site with the new flooring.

The purchase, transportation, and reassembly of the doors transformed Ruskin Park's dance hall and auditorium into a state-of-the-art and elegant structure. This move ensured Ruskin Park's spot in the local dance culture and kept the property vital through the two world wars and into the 1950s. Big names, including Lawrence Welk, the Everly Brothers, and Conway Twitty, appeared at Ruskin Park (Ruskin Park Hunting Club, 2015). The property's long history with music saw it inducted into the South Dakota Rock and Roll Hall of Fame in 2010.

Ruskin Park is well documented as it was a huge project affecting thousands of people. The drive to the park could be an adventure in itself on dry dirt, or with luck, on gravel roads. Early, however, autos often had to navigate roads that were more like trails—rutted, muddy, and full of potholes. Given the distance from large cities, such as Sioux Falls forty-five miles away, 500 cars was still a really substantial number back then.

An article by Ruskin Park Hunting Club provides more information:

> We have been operating Ruskin Park Hunting since 2003, but Ruskin Park history dates back to the days of Dakota Territory. The Ruskin Park area was an intersection of pioneer and Sioux Indian culture. Because of the location of an ancient river ford on the James River, three pioneer wagon trails met here and it became a gathering place for early settlers.
>
> A popular recreation area, Ruskin Park grew to include a hotel, cabins, a theater, a baseball diamond, tennis courts, and a golf course. A mile-long racetrack for horses and cars was considered one of the fastest and best tracks in the United States. An

airstrip for air exhibitions and a bandstand were provided. Canoeing, horseshoes, and basketball were also enjoyed. (2015)

In addition, photographs prove that some of the best teams of the US Black Baseball League frequently competed at the park in the early days of the 1900s.

Ruskin Park antiques at the Zoss "Ruskin Park" Hunting Lodge

An additional paragraph in the *Sanborn Weekly Journal* adds the following:

In 1915, after improvements to the racetrack were made, a 50-mile auto race was scheduled for July 3 and 5 with a $500 prize for the winners. A 25-mile motorcycle race was also held with $100 prize. In August of 1919, the State Carnival of Sports was held in honor of World War I veterans, who enjoyed free admission that day. The event featured the Donaldson Brothers Flying Circus complete with three army biplanes with rapid-fire machine guns performing acrobatic stunts, loop the loops, formation flying and spiral drops. Auto races, a baseball game, a barbecue, band music and dancing were all part of the day's festivities.

The Roaring Twenties saw changes in society and advances in travel and left Ruskin Park to settle into hosting mostly local events such as county picnics, political meetings, Fourth of July celebrations and the weekly crowd at the dance pavilion. Bands such as Lawrence Welk were favorites of the time, laying at events named the "Garden Dance," "Harvest Moon Dance" and "Hunters Ball." The '20s were when writer Tom Barkdull described Ruskin Park as "The Playground of the Prairie," and racecar driver Eddie Rickenbacker allegedly remarked that the Ruskin Park racetrack was the fastest dirt track he had ever driven.

The Grandstand at the Ruskin Park racetrack and ballpark was packed on many an occasion [with the audience] watching everything from horse, car and motorcycle races to local baseball teams battling it out. (Admin, 2013, pp. 5-6)

Uncle Herb's catch on the James River, Ruskin Park, South Dakota

Interesting speculations of events in the early part of the 1900s can be linked to descriptions of the park activity. Specifically, the crowds were huge, and the park was very well and widely known, not only locally in Sanborn County but around South Dakota and in nearby states. Through newspaper stories and personal accounts, we know that political rallies and speeches commonly took place at the park; as a result, it's reasonable to speculate that Ben Millard and Senator Norbeck had met each other earlier. At a minimum, because of the significance of Ruskin Park in South Dakota, these two very literate men had likely read something of the others' records in the news.

Ben's experience in managing, marketing, financing, and developing the park and its wide list of activities, along with his partner, Dowdell, was an incredibly important asset to have when he arrived at the Badlands and began working with Senator Norbeck on developing an infrastructure to attract thousands of visitors not just to drive through but to stay and enjoy seeing and learning all about the Badlands.

The Ruskin Park operation was a mammoth event in Ben's life that also created indelible memories for his children. Of course, many of the aspects of developing and managing the park transferred to his efforts with the Badlands. About the day-to-day operations of the park, Ben Zoss told me that he had been able to go through some of the buildings and was able to answer my questions as to how, for example, the park provided for all the people when there were big events. For one thing, he confirmed that a long building was set at an angle to the racetrack that was like a barracks inside with a whole series of closed-in toilets on both the men's and women's side. The basement of the hotel also housed a large pump with a huge flywheel that pumped water to the barracks and the hotel.

As we were talking about how the accommodations for all those, at times, thousands of visitors and residents, Zoss explained how Ben managed the operations on a daily basis, handled the financing, set the schedules for the races, and directed the various employees. Zoss even found some documents concerning the races that showed Ben was the first line manager.

Ruskin Park Tryouts for World Record, Auto Races

The first time I met Zoss, through an introduction by Joe Tlustos who was then with South Dakota Public Radio and TV, he asked me if I would research a meeting my grandfather was said to have had with the president of the NW Dirt Track Auto Association. Zoss had the name of the president, and, in Ruskin Park lore, it was said the meeting took place in midsummer 1924 in Mitchell, South Dakota.

Ben Zoss in former Ruskin Park, South Dakota,
with antique sewing machine collection.

The purpose of the meeting was to see if Ben could secure approval to rerun, officially, a replacement trial for the world's record one-mile at Ruskin Park. When the original race had been run on the Fourth of July at Ruskin, an accident caused the race to be canceled, and the track had to be closed for wall and track repair.

With the very capable help of my close friend and associate, Richard Layne, who is the head of the audiovisual department at the Institute of Historical Survey Foundation in Las Cruces, New Mexico, we started "digging" (well, Richard dug as he is so proficient at it, and I watched). He spent hours over three to four days foraging through old newspapers and other writings to see if we could prove or disprove the story of the meeting. Although we couldn't find anything directly about the meeting, we did find substantial proof that the meeting took place and that Ruskin Park was given permission to reschedule the race for Labor Day in 1924. We found a newspaper article titled, "Labor Day Auto Races at Ruskin Park" in the *Mitchell South Dakota Evening Republican*, which describes the steps taken to repair the track and to get ready for the Labor Day race:

> The Speedway at Ruskin Park is fast coming into shape for the big Labor Day race which will be next Monday September 1st. Arrangements are being made to sprinkle the track to hold [down] on the dust and with the turn, [increase the] bank from 10 to 13 feet. Together with the fastest cars of the country there remains but little doubt that the world's record will be lowered. This track now has a record of 3 seconds of the world's record, which was made by Mr. John McCoy a national driver last 4th of July. Mr. McCoy feels confident with [the] track sprinkled and the south turn back 3 feet higher that he will have no trouble in lowering the world's record.

> There will be a program on Sunday, August 1st, consisting of a ball game between Lechter and Howard, followed by the elimination, preliminary, and world record trial races [that] are preparatory for the big Labor Day races.

It is expected that many people will avail themselves of all the free camping privileges, arriving Saturday and remaining over until after the Labor Day races.

In a repeat of the above article by a different newspaper (*The Evening Huronite*,), an additional column describes the actual trial races at Ruskin Park. Interesting comments and details of the results of the race are written as well:

The [trial] race was called off [due to the accident], the winners being decided on the way in which they had finished up in that time period. JJ McCoy of Ortonville Minnesota No. 3, who finished 6th in the Indianapolis Speedway contest recently, won the race as he did practically all the others of the afternoon with Brakhage of Webster in his Duisenberg, number 19 finishing second and Battig third.

In the first event of the afternoon at 3 miles try out, Battig set the track record of a mile in 51 seconds. McCoy in a special won the 5, then the 10th and the 25-mile events. Dresselhuys of Wagner, number 17 in a Dodge special finish second in the 10-mile event. . . . Seventeen cars entered the first event, 12 qualifying for the remainder of the races. The final consolation race was called off on account of the accident.

It is estimated that fully ten thousand people were seated in the grandstand or parked in their cars around the natural arena around the Ruskin Park mile track. The races were about the best thing I've ever been witnessed in the state and with the announcement that the track will be either oiled or treated with a chemical to keep down the dust before the Labor Day races come, predictions are general that Ruskin

Park will develop the fastest mile track in the entire United States within another year or so.

The dances in the evening were well patronized, but the boxing card was said to have been mediocre. Hundreds of cars from Huron attended the races in the afternoon, renewing acquaintances with Ben Millard, who is running the park. The day all in all was a decided success. (Labor Day Auto Races at Ruskin Park, 1924, September 2)

By this time, Ben, Stella, and their three children—Glen, Faye, and Herbert—had moved to Whittier, California, but they still came back to their beloved park in South Dakota for the summers.

After that, the information lines concerning racing at Ruskin Park and attempts to set a world record went dead! What we did find, however, was an article about a driver in Minnesota who had set the world record sometime before the proposed Labor Day event at Ruskin Park. Unfortunately, that seemed to settle the Ruskin Park trial attempt to set a new world record.

One of the areas not yet touched on here at any length involved the auditorium and outdoor stage performances. These memories I can recall now on the part of my father regarding his interests that caused him such pleasure to work on when my sisters and I were quite young in the 1930s. He often wanted to put on "stage performances" in our house and record them, using early versions of tape recordings and film.

From Ruskin Park, there is a well-publicized picture on several web pages showing the park's history. For example, in the "'Playground of the Prairie' memorialized with historic marker" article in the *Sanborn Weekly Journal* for 2013 (p. 6), there is a photograph showing "An

ORCHESTRA stayed on permanently for a time at the Park, so that dances could be easily planned." Seated in front, on the last of three steps up to the bandstand step, the young man on the left is my father, Glen E. Millard, who served as director of plays many times at the park.

Dad had "perfect pitch" and could listen to nearly any song or musical recording and guess what key the piece was in. He'd then go to the piano and, about 95 percent of the time, be able to hit exactly the right key for the note he had quoted for the piece. He couldn't read music, but if someone played a few chords or notes from a song or piece of music, he could play chords immediately and catch the melody of the piece. I suppose, over the years, we heard and saw my father do that hundreds of times.

He never took music lessons. All his musical ability came from his days at Ruskin Park. He would have been fourteen years old when Grandfather became owner of the park. Dad attended Artesian High School, and, certainly, he and our family would have gone to the park even before Grandfather and Dowdell became its owners.

Beyond that, however, my father's great interest was as a director and actor, which he carried from his Ruskin Park days to Whittier High School in Whittier, California, where he was a very active member of the Black Friars stage production company.

A rather long article about a play was reported in the *Weekly State Spirit* of Huron, South Dakota, in which my grandfather acted and my father both acted and directed. With apologies to the reader for occasional repetitions later, I have included some of these accounts to back up my personal opinions of how I saw my father and grandfather working together as a family unit. That characteristic of the Millard family carried forward to the Badlands days during both the good and very tough times and is one of the main reasons Grandfather and his family were the right people at the right time and in the right place to meet the challenges involved in helping to protect the Badlands.[7]

The title of the article in the *Weekly State Spirit* was "GOOD PRODUCTION WAS GIVEN—Ruskin Park Players in 'He Fell in Love with His Wife' Excellent."

> The theatrical season was opened at the Grand last evening. The Ruskin Park stock company presenting the comedy drama called "He Fell in Love with His Wife."
>
> The play which is laid in and near the city of Syracuse, N.Y., is the story of a young farmer, who, in order to prevent scandal in the neighborhood, marries his housekeeper. The marriage is purely a business agreement between the man and woman, who live together for a year before they realize they love each other. . . . The leading comedy character was Mrs. Mump, a former housekeeper for James Holcroft, the farmer. . . . The character of Justice Harkins was well taken by Mr. Ben Millard. The part of Henry Ferguson was portrayed by Mr. Glen Millard, whose work would equal that of a professional. The part, which is that of a villain, is, by no means, an easy one to play, and Mr. Millard is deserving of much praise in the able way in which he handled it. Taken altogether the play was very good, every member of the cast being perfect in his lines. Mr. Glen Millard under whose direction the play was produced should be given much of the credit for his work in drilling a cast of amateur players to produce a play in the professional manner in which it was played last evening. Although last evening's

---

[7] Now that I'm older it's curious to observe how dad and grandfather worked together. As director, dad would give grandfather, a renowned orator, instructions on how to act. Grandfather would then accept the advice.

performance was small, every person present enjoyed every moment of the play. The piece will be presented again this evening, and the company should be greeted by a packed house for the play is well worth seeing. (1915)

A second newspaper account is equally, if perhaps not more, relevant to Grandfather's personal abilities, which proved so necessary to the work that would be required of him in the Badlands. Much of his later job required giving presentations, speeches, remarks, and longer comments to Cedar Pass Lodge guests and visitors, politicians, ranchers, and administrators of one federal or state department or another.

A newspaper account of a historic speech given by Grandfather presents a good example of one of several reviews of his other speeches found in historical archives or more current history files. The following article in the *Woonsocket News,* May 22nd, 1975, is a remembrance of a long-past Memorial Day celebration:

> In the afternoon, a patriotic program was held in Theinsens Opera House. One such program was most memorable to me. Usually one of the Fitch Brothers reads the Declaration of Independence the major "speech" of the day. But this year he was away at school. A newcomer had come to be a business citizen of Artesian. Mr. Ben Millard, the new banker had a flair for oratory. His deep and sonorous voice, began impressively: "Four score and seven years ago, our fathers brought forth upon this continent a new nation, conceived in Liberty and dedicated to the proposition that all men are created equal."
>
> I think that was my first exposure to a patriotic emotion. I haven't really listened to those words before. I was spellbound. As Mr. Millard went on through those historic

words, he became more dramatic in his delivery. When he reached the soul-stirring words of the conclusion—"that we here highly resolve that these dead shall not have died in vain, that this nation, under God shall have a new birth of freedom, and that the government of the people, by the people and for the people shall not perish from the earth" I was fascinated: I sat in silent appreciation of the impact of those words. I think it was the first time I had heard it recited. Mr. Millard did not read it, nor did he use notes. It was almost like hearing Mr. Lincoln first pronounce that address. (We Called It Decoration Day, Too, 1975)

Described in the article as a new "business citizen of Artesian" and "the new banker," Ben gave the speech in 1898 or early 1899, when he was 28 or 29 years old. He had just moved his family of three to Artesian when he was offered the opportunity to manage the bank owned by his friend, W. A. Loveland.

After that, even before he became one of the owners and managers of Ruskin Park in 1910, he would have had plenty of opportunities to introduce himself to groups and individuals as the "new man and family in town."

Becoming the new co-owner of Ruskin Park was such a giant step forward in the community that he must have been involved in many situations that called for making remarks, speaking, and giving all sorts of presentations.

Ben was also well known for his artistic presentations and large marketing or welcome displays, which he learned about and displayed in Ruskin Park, as described in the March 14th, 1924,

Evening Huronite (Huron, South Dakota) article titled "'Auditorium Is Real Fairyland', Millard Shows Real Talent in Decorations for Spring Exposition Now On":

> Never before in the history of Huron has the Daum auditorium looked as beautiful as it does today. Ben Millard of Ruskin Park summer resort doing himself proud in the decorations he has put up for the fourth annual Spring Exposition. The balcony has been continued around [the] entire room for uniformity and each booth is set off with lattice work and paneling, all in white with an abundance of green similax to add the touch of color while artificial flowers and numerous singing canaries concealed in the similax in simplex add beauty for both the eye and ear to appreciate. The Exhibitors' booths are all uniform and highly artistic, showing from the right around the hall, displays by the Standard Radiator Company, the Huron Marble and Granite Works, two displays by the Huron Light and Power Company, Morin and Colten Wholesale Grocers [continuing with a list of fifteen or twenty more companies and ending with a number of automobile-related companies' latest auto models on display]. ("Auditorium Is Real Fairyland", 1924)

Including the days when Ben and family lived in Artesian and Huron but also after he had retired to California, which, as referred to in earlier chapters, would have been sometime around 1910,[8] the family was still actively engaged in stage performances over the summers at Ruskin Park. They were really attached to the park and loved putting on plays. In my father's box of old documents, I found unused colored stationery with the heading, "Ruskin Park Stock

---

[8] At some later time, after the family had been retired in California, they had also lived in Denver, Colorado, but once again, traveled back to South Dakota during the summers.

Company Playing Latest and Best Royalty Plays, Each Production Elaborately Produced. PLAYING SUMMER ENGAGEMENT AT SOUTH DAKOTA'S MOST POPULAR SUMMER RESORT, RUSKIN, PARK, FORESTBURG, SOUTH DAKOTA."

The three names running across the top of the page in small print, left to right, are B. H. Millard, President; G. E. Millard, Manager; and R. E. Dowdell, Treasurer. The address shown is "Winter Headquarters. Los Angeles, Cal."

It turns out that they had even hired a motion picture producer who came with them to Ruskin Park with the intention to produce some movies to show around the country. As reported in an online article, the following short paragraph confirms what I had also found elsewhere:

A motion picture house was built with stage to enable the presentation of home-talent plays, Mr. Millard was a natural actor as were his children Faye, Glen and Herbert. They brought a director from Whittier and a traveling company was formed. That however, was of short duration. . . . For a few seasons the theater personnel lived there free during rehearsals of the plays presented under the direction of Alma Swain of Whittier, Calif., with Louis Foster of the same city taking major parts. Ben Millard and his son, Glen Millard served in double capacity, as managers and leading actors.

Perhaps the popular comedy "Charlie's Aunt" was their most ambitious production. Remembered by the participants for fun during preparations was [greater] than the production. Those were truly the days of Ruskin Park. (The Story of Ruskin Park, 1975)

The above paragraphs confirm a number of essential facts in piecing together bits of the family story. First, in our family over the years, I had heard remarks or conversations regarding Grandfather's abilities, and this article is a further indication of how good an actor and speaker Grandfather was. Second, the article confirmed my conclusions on how well the family worked together. All three children and Grandfather could and did frequently work together as a family unit in situations that were unique to their world. Putting one's self on the stage or in film acting situations for others to see is not a comfortable place for many of us. Third, it confirms that the Millards had moved or retired to California and yet continued to come back to Ruskin Park in the summers.

A fourth observation was made with the help of rancher Ben Zoss, who in a recent telephone interview described how there was a big pump with a really large flywheel in the basement of the hotel at the park, which supplied cold water to locations in the park from the four artesian wells that had been dug. Grandfather had to lay out the specs and decide where the pump would be located.

Ruskin Park was described in such detail in this chapter because I feel that here is where Ben made the critical discovery that he had the ability to manage others. With so many different but critical jobs now at stake, and later required of him in his Badland's work, the importance of honing these skills cannot be overstated.

The following paragraph indicates one of the most critical aspects of Ben's demonstrated management abilities:

Stables for the horses and bleachers for the viewers were constructed. Later auto races took the place of horses. Grandstands augmented the bleachers. William Dowdell also had oversight of these additions. A launch, canoes and boats and bathhouses added activities as well as tennis courts, diving boards and a rustic bridge. Mr. and Mrs. Walt Starr ran a concession stand and he overlooked the care of horses and the upkeep of the mile dirt track, built with saucered rims. Eddie Rickenbacker remarked that it was the fastest dirt track he had ever driven. Other named racers competed and sportsmen from far and wide came for the sports that Ruskin Park offered. (The Story of Ruskin Park, 1975)

Finally, this same article points out that the bust years in the farm community from 1919 into the 1930s had a severe domino effect on other areas such as entertainment and therefore Ruskin Park. The period hit farmers with a triple whammy: first, the farmland bust beginning in 1919 and continuing through the Great Depression of 1929 into the 1930s; second, the incredible grasshopper plague; and, third, the Dust Bowl years. The combined effect was so severe that a chapter can only partially recall the misery so many faced. However, those years had favorable aspects for Ben's efforts in protecting the Badlands.

The article by the *Sanborn Weekly Journal* records, with good photos, information about the park, including the inscription on the historic plaque for Ruskin Park:

Ruskin Park was synonymous with excitement, entertainment and romance from its inception.

The area's first pioneers settled along the James River near here in 1873. Santee and Rodee families homesteaded south of here, near a large grove (Rodee's Grove), where picnics, political rallies and community gatherings were held.

In 1902, Hiram A. Rodee Jr. cleared part of the grove and built a two-story hotel, a lunchroom, stables and other buildings; erected a large canvas auditorium; and named the park after poet and naturalist John Ruskin. Special trains brought thousands of people to this site, the parking entrance depot. People built or rented cottages and tents for summer camping. Chautauquas, plays, programs, meetings and picnics soon made Ruskin Park the cultural and entertainment center of Sanborn County.

In 1910 Robert E. Dowdell and Ben H. Millard purchased the park and [as mentioned earlier] made further improvements, adding a theater, forty cabins, and one of the fastest one-mile racetracks around, still visible on satellite images. Over the years, many local and nationally famous bands played to hundreds in the glass dance pavilion.

Later park proprietors were Marion C. Dowdell, 1930–1949, Don Shaw, 1949–1954; and Walter and Dagmar Siegenthaler, 1954–1968.[9]

Forty-six years after the last pair of feet jitterbugged across the well-worn maple floor of the dance hall down by the Jim [James River], those who still hold the memories dear gathered near the river Saturday to commemorate and celebrate the famed playground of their youth. (Admin, 2013)

---

[9] Wording listed on the new historic plaque (viewable online).

SECTION 2: "THE BUST" – EAST RIVER COUNTRY

Chapter 5: Farmland Market Bust and Grasshopper Plagues

The smooth sailing, high profits, low-to-zero income taxes all disappeared in the 1920s for farmers and ranchers ahead of and continuing through the Great Depression of 1929 and well into what's frequently referred to in various publications as the "Dirty Thirties" (the Dust Bowl years of the 1930s). Few people outside the Midwest know that the Great Depression started a full nine years early here:

> In the 1920s, as the afterglow of wartime prosperity ended, the U.S. Government incrementally withdrew support of wheat prices and overseas production resumed. Domestic wheat prices plummeted, while taxes and prices of consumer goods rose. Although improved mechanization made farming more efficient, and farmers were able to place more acres were [sic] under production, many of the farmers who had bought land during the war-time boom were still unable to keep up with payments. South Dakota and the rural Midwest plunged into economic depression [in 1920]. . . . In South Dakota alone, 174 banks failed by 1925. Midwestern congressional representatives made unsuccessful attempts to pass legislation aimed at helping farmers, and bad went to worse after the stock market collapse in October 1929. Commodity prices again plunged . . . During this time railroads also constricted, hit hard by the economy and growing popularity of automobiles, which threatened the railroad's monopoly on

transportation. . . . The stock market crash was accompanied by the onset of regional drought and the consequences of decades of environmental degradation. (SWCA Environmental Consultants, 2013, p. 21)

Many readers will remember hearing about the Great Depression and the Dust Bowl years, which have been the subject of a fine documentary by Ken Burns. But we can't forget the third fork of the triple whammy that farmers in the Dakotas experienced—a grasshopper plague!

The following quote from an article in the *Capital Journal* newspaper in South Dakota in 2015 recounts a situation that is still difficult to comprehend:

It's one of the things the late Henry Hewlett couldn't forget about growing up in the Great Depression in the town of Canning, South Dakota—not just dust and drought, but grasshoppers. Grasshoppers filled the air like winged weather and clattered like living hailstones against every surface.

"It's kind of uphill for the train coming up into Canning. There were so many grasshoppers on the tracks that the engine spun out and couldn't pull the train," he recalled. "So they unhooked two cars and come in and got them ahead of the engine. They would crush the grasshoppers ahead of the engine so it could pull the train." (Nixon, 2015)

Hewlett remembered them [grasshoppers] flitting overhead like a glittering cloud that came between him and the sun. [Bruce] Helbig [retired USDA entomologist] said Hewlett's memory of grasshoppers darkening the sun is believable . . . there are pilots' accounts of encountering this species [*Melanoplus sanguinipes*] at 2,000 to 9,000 feet above the ground. . . . Henry Hewlett used to refer to those grasshoppers he met as a boy in South Dakota [as] "locusts." But those grasshoppers of the 1930s weren't locusts. The one true locust of North America was the insect that devastated South Dakota and other parts of the Midwest and Plaines in the 1860s and the 1870s—the Rocky Mountain Locust (*Melanoplus spretis*). It is now extinct. It was last observed in 1902 in southern Canada.

It made for the kind of incident from the first half of the 1930s that Hewlett remembered vividly when he visited the Capital Journal at the start of 2015. . . . The grasshoppers would eat anything—not only the gardens, but also the varnish off the handles of the garden tools. "If you'd leave a shovel or a fork sticking up in the yard, next morning the handle would be rough. They'd eat all of it . . .," Hewlett said.

Entomologists agree that conditions were ideal for grasshoppers—at least in the early years of that dry decade. . . . Dr. Robert E. Pfadt, an authority on grasshoppers in the western United States, found that particularly true in the Dakotas. . . . "Populations increased slowly for three years, 1928 to 1930. Both species reached phenomenal numbers in 1931 and 1932. They devastated fields of alfalfa, small grains, corn, vegetables, and a variety of fruit and shelterbelt trees." (Nixon, 2015)

This second section of this book, "The Bust" – East River Country, reminded me of a famous World War I doughboy song, "There's a Long, Long Trail," as I wrote of the beginning of the long Depression:

Nights are growing very lonely,

Days are very long.

I'm a-growing weary only

List'ning for your song.

Old remembrances are thronging

Thro' my memory

Till it seems the world is full of dreams

Just to call you back to me.

Most people remember this song for its chorus:

There's a long, long trail a-winding

Into the land of my dreams,

Where the nightingales are singing

And the white moon beams.

There's a long, long night of waiting

Until my dreams all come true;

Till the day when I'll be going down

That long, long trail with you (There's a Long Long Trail A-Winding, 1915)

A very good summary of the situation that confronted Ben and his family was written by the staff of National Reserve Life Insurance in the brochure made for his funeral services:

Now we enter upon a period of years which proved the mettle of Ben Millard's character. Following World War I and in the early twenties, farm property declined greatly and bank failures became to be frequent occurrences throughout the area. As a result of this economic cycle, Ben Millard saw his work of many years vanish in practically complete financial loss. But courage and fortitude mark the man—Ben Millard continued to work and joining the South Dakota State Banking Department, he was assigned the difficult task of working with banks which had either been closed or were being considered for closing. Once again in the banking field, he was involved in work he knew and loved and his years of experience and understanding of the financial problems of banks enabled him to create a procedure for handling distressed banks which was destined to become the official formula used by the South Dakota State Department of Banking. (1956)

In effect, the South Dakota State Banking Department attributed to Ben a system for handling distressed banks that could be called the "Ben Millard Stressed Bank Procedure." The system was necessary because the situation for banks in South Dakota was severe, as one can imagine, with farmland and crops being devastated.

The stock market crash was accompanied by the onset of regional drought and the consequences of decades of environmental degradation. The summer of 1930, which was the second driest in the history of the state, was characterized by baked-hardpan fields that were impenetrable by the little moisture that managed to reach the ground. By 1933, dust storms, "black blizzards," raged with now-legendary intensity, with the Dakotas forming the northernmost edge of the Dust Bowl. (SWCA Environmental Consultants, 2013, pp. 21-22)

South Dakota farmers were devastated. Farmers fed thistles to cattle and watched helplessly as grasshoppers devoured anything that grew—not just crops and gardens, but even the leaves and bark from trees. Chickens remained a somewhat reliable food source, but the dust storms killed them too.

Journalist Lorena Hickok, working for the Federal Emergency Relief Administration (FERA) in 1933, wrote of South Dakota, "A more hopeless place I never saw." [They were] held hostage by egregiously high interest rates and the consequences of their own mistreatment of the natural environment. (SWCA Environmental Consultants, 2013, p. 22)

A further description of early homesteaders' practices, which reflected their lack of understanding of the prairie and the need for dryland farming techniques, is given in relation to the resulting Dust Bowl:

The Dust Bowl [also known as the Dirty Thirties] was a period of severe dust storms that greatly damaged the ecology and agriculture of the American and Canadian Prairies during the 1930s; severe drought and a failure to apply dryland farming methods to prevent the aeolian processes (wind erosion) caused the phenomenon. The drought came in three waves, 1934, 1936, and 1939–1940, but some regions of the high plains experienced drought conditions for as many as eight years. With insufficient understanding of the ecology of the plains, farmers had conducted extensive deep plowing of the virgin topsoil of the Great Plains during the previous decade; this had displaced the native, deep-rooted grasses that normally trapped soil and moisture even during periods of drought and high winds. The rapid mechanization of farm equipment, especially small gasoline tractors, and widespread use of the combine harvester contributed to farmers' decisions to convert arid grassland (much of which received no more than 10 inches (~250 mm) of precipitation per year) to cultivated cropland.

During the drought of the 1930s, the unanchored soil turned to dust, which the prevailing winds blew away in huge clouds that sometimes blackened the sky. These choking billows of dust—named "black blizzards" or "black rollers"—traveled cross country, reaching as far as the East Coast and striking such cities as New York City and Washington, D.C. On the plains, they often reduced visibility to 3 feet (1 m) or less. Associated Press reporter Robert E. Geiger happened to be in Boise City, Oklahoma, to witness the "Black Sunday" black blizzards of April 14, 1935; Edward Stanley, Kansas City news editor of the Associated Press coined the term "Dust Bowl" while rewriting Geiger's news story. While the term "the Dust Bowl" was originally a reference to the geographical area affected by the dust, today it usually refers to the event itself. (Dust bowl, n.d.)

I can remember my father, while we were on pheasant hunting trips in the mid-1940s, talking about how poor farmers had to scrounge for food. He said that in the fall, during bird migrations south, a farmer would wait until huge flocks of blackbirds settled in barren trees near their house. Then, because shotgun shells were expensive for farmers with barely sufficient income for their families, the farmer would sneak up to the tree and line up as many blackbirds as possible for a single shot.

I can also remember hunting pals who were ten or twelve years my senior telling me stories of doing the same thing with ducks in areas where there was a little water in some bluffs or dwindled sloughs. And, although as young hunters they wanted to learn to shoot ducks flying, when they had only been given three shells, they had better be sure to come home with several ducks or be prepared to catch hell from their fathers. If they wasted a shell or two shooting at flying ducks, they might have to lie on their stomachs for a couple hours waiting for some more ducks so they could carefully line up several in their sites on the water to kill as many as they could at once with the one shell they had left.[10]

One more source of food or money in South Dakota was jackrabbits. In some areas, they were plentiful. I learned about them when my wife and I lived in Huron, where my grandfather and his family had lived earlier. In the very late fall and winter, their pelts became valuable to the furrier trade after the hides turned white for winter camouflage (as Lewis and Clark found out). Around 1954, I hunted these jackrabbits, and there was a place in town near the railroad depot that the frozen carcasses could be dropped off for two or three dollars each (now, a cured, good white hide is worth about $11). In just a couple hours, driving slowly on back roads with a .22 rifle and a scope, it was easy to get several, take them home, and pile them up in the unheated garage to freeze solid. I remember buying a bottle or two of good Irish whiskey for Christmas with jackrabbit earnings.

The Lewis and Clark Expedition discovered this rabbit as one of their new species:

> On September 14th, 1804, while traveling through what is now western South Dakota, the Corps of Discovery encountered a creature they had never seen before. William Clark wrote in his Journal: "Shields killed hare weighing 6 1/2 lb: verry [sic] pore, the head narrow and its ears 3 Inches wide and 6 long, from the fore to the end of the hindfoot is 2 feet 11 inch. Hite [height] 1 foot 1 3/4 its tail long and thick white, clearly the mountain Hare of Europe."

---

[10] Conversation with my friend, Francis Laska.

It was not, however, the mountain hare of Europe but unique animal known today as the white-tailed jackrabbit. The white-tailed jackrabbit is found throughout west-central Canada and the northwestern United States. Not to be confused with its southwestern cousin, the black-tailed jackrabbit, the white-tailed variety is the second-largest hare in North America.

To Lewis and Clark, this was no ordinary rabbit. Accustomed to the eastern cottontail—which weighs all of a pound—they were surprised to encounter a hare of such impressive size—moreover one that changed color in the seasons. On January 3, 1805, Private Joseph Whitehouse wrote, "One of the hunters killed a beautiful white hare, which is common in this Country." The Corps had noticed that the animals changed from summer grey to winter white, the better to camouflage themselves against the snow at Fort Mandan. (Hunter, 2010)

On a personal note, when we hunted in areas where there were bits of water and trees, somehow Dad and other friends always seemed to find out which farmers still had operating moonshine stills so my father and my uncle could sample the local white lightning, or moonshine. Those were some of the pluses or unintended consequences of the Prohibition days of 1920 to 1933. Farmers were struggling in those days, and when I first went hunting in 1938 or 1939, their sources of revenue in some cases were still being refreshed or aged by distillation practices learned in those really dry economic years.[11] My uncles on Mother's side

---

[11] Prohibition was all but sealed by the time the United States entered World War I in 1917, but the conflict served as one of the last nails in the coffin of legalized alcohol. Dry advocates argued that the barley used in brewing beer could be made into bread to feed American soldiers and war-ravaged Europeans, and they succeeded in winning wartime bans on strong drink. Anti-alcohol crusaders were often fueled by xenophobia, and the war allowed them to paint America's largely German brewing industry as a threat. "We have German enemies in this

were of German extraction and had been in the liquor business before Prohibition. In St. Paul and Minneapolis, there was a very good grapevine network of where to go. Those "watering holes" are well documented, and it's still easy to learn from declining members of the older generation where the good places were to refurbish a tired and wounded spirit or to celebrate.

You'll notice that the writings and numerous quotes in this section are devoted to describing outside forces, Ben's point of view, and situations over which he had no control. However, those forces not only describe the situation in which his fortune in agricultural land, and also any remaining interests he may have had in Ruskin Park, suffered, but they reflect the negative economic conditions he suddenly had to deal with.

The interesting part is how those same negative forces, and his experiences in dealing with them in this period of his life, resulted in a 180-degree turn from negative to positive when he encountered different tasks in the Badlands.

In the latter part of the 1920s, he first began his career in the Badlands when the grasshopper plague, the drought, and the dust bowl were severely affecting farmers and their land. All those domino effects coincidentally made him the right person for the right job at the right time. As it turned out, that was the same time Senator Norbeck urgently needed a trusted assistant for the quest to protect the Badlands.

Therefore, one final element of the drastic economic downfall that Ben was facing needs a bit of perspective. First, in 1917, as the National Reserve Life Insurance memorial brochure

---

country, too," one temperance politician argued. "And the worst of all our German enemies, the most treacherous, the most menacing, are Pabst, Schlitz, Blatz and Miller." (10 Things You Should Know about Prohibition, Evan Andrews, History.com)

mentions, he had disposed of much of his banking interests to become a senior partner in a substantial real estate firm. That was two years in advance of the bottom falling out in the beginning of the agricultural land depression.

In old newspaper archives, I found an advertisement for South Dakota land for sale. The real estate firm of Millard-Kyes-Haskell, 18 Wisconsin Street, Huron, South Dakota, ran a large ad offering a coupon for a free bulletin about the latest opportunities in South Dakota land in a Des Moines, Iowa, magazine:

> If you are a prospective purchaser of land either for a home or an investment this Bulletin will be of great value to you. It contains the best offerings bought early in 10 counties. It brings to you the results of capable buyers who are in the territory the year around. Fill in the coupon and mail it today. (Advertisement, 1919)

South Dakota banks began to fail in large numbers in the mid-1920s after the agricultural land market hit the skids beginning in 1919. The story often heard within our family goes as follows:

As noted earlier, Grandfather had decided to "winter" in Whittier, California, starting around 1907. My uncle, Herb Millard, said that "by 1920, Boy (Grandfather) probably figured himself worth $1,500,000. He had land for 10 miles down the road, but he didn't own it properly. He had a partner, A. M. Haskell." While at home in California, a late mislaid or earlier lost telegram arrived from his real estate partner, Haskell, advising Grandfather that a large parcel of farmland had just come to Haskell's attention. Haskell thought they should immediately buy it because it was a particularly good piece of property at the right price. In those days, communications were limited to mail or telegrams as telephones were not reliable, at least in rural areas.[12] Whatever happened with the communications between Grandfather and Haskell, the family story I heard was that unfortunately Grandfather did not receive the message in time, and Haskell already completed the transaction to buy the land. In the interim between when Haskell closed the purchase transaction for Millard-Kyes-Haskell and when Grandfather finally received the message, the bottom had dropped out of the real estate market. As a result, the value of the land was underwater, and Grandfather had financially been about cleaned out.

Banks, especially small agricultural banks in rural areas, were hard hit and failing, and several within the Badlands area were on the edge of failing or had already succumbed. The South Dakota Banking Department urgently needed advisers with knowledge and skills in the banking business, particularly those with heavy deposits in agriculture.

Once again, it turned out that Grandfather's experience was just what they were looking for, and, of course, with the banks he had owned and run, he especially fit the bill.

---

[12] According to online information on the history of telephone communications in rural South Dakota, telephone lines were not laid in many areas until the 1950s. In rural southeastern South Dakota, the Rural Electrical Association (REA) laid 2,000 lines in 1949. When I began spending extended periods of time at Cedar Pass Lodge in the mid-1940s, the only nearby telephone was at Joe and Mabel Haight's hardware store in Interior, South Dakota. Using a party line with a crank phone to reach the operator, I would request a long-distance call to speak with my parents back in St. Paul, Minnesota. It might take half an hour or longer to put through a call, and the lines were not great. (anonymous) https://history.sd.gov/museum/docs/SouthDakotaCommunicates.pdf

SECTION 3: "THE BADLANDS EPIC" – WEST RIVER COUNTRY

Chapter 6: Ben Millard Meets the Badlands and Senator Norbeck

After following Ben's path in life up to this point, it would seem that there was a spirit, perhaps a strong Native American Spirit or just some kind of a powerful, mystical energy, that pulled Ben to the Badlands in 1927. That possibility only seems more plausible after hearing of his trail from here on! But leading up to this point, the coincidence of Ben's arrivals at various waypoints on his trek, loaded with current experience and knowledge exactly fitting what was needed at that particular place and time, just kept piling up. Many of these observances remind me of long conversations I had with rancher Ben Zoss about Ben's career back in the Ruskin Park days from the mid-1890s to 1924. Ben Zoss, my recording partner Richard Varco, and I agreed that the coincidences seemed to line up, such as the fire during Ben's first year at Shenandoah College in Iowa that destroyed the campus and sent him to Lincoln, Nebraska. Once there, he somehow met W. A. Loveland and, as just a nineteen-year-old college sophomore, was given the opportunity to enter the banking business at Loveland's bank in Lesterville, South Dakota.[13]

The fascinating coincidences didn't stop there; they just kept piling up to arrange Ben's first visit to the Badlands in the spring of 1927. A fine and thorough book called *A Revelation Called the*

---

[13] At this point in marking waypoints along Ben's trail to the Badlands, it's necessary for me to make a statement for full disclosure: although I am not a strong believer in the occult or science fiction, I do subscribe to the theory that energy doesn't just disappear—it changes form.

Badlands: Building a National Park 1909 to 1939 was written by a senior Badlands park ranger, Jay Shuler, who did a huge amount of careful research on old government, Senator Norbeck's letters, and other files on the Badlands. Ranger Shuler's short book is a staple reference for anyone interested in the incredible travails of creating a national monument or national park, which are now up against powerful and determined forces to prevent such protections or tear them down, often only for short-term, temporary gains.

From old letters, Ranger Shuler established the date of Ben's first visit to the Badlands in the spring of 1927:

> Unusually successful in early ventures, [Ben] Millard's fortune eroded in early 1920s when the farm depression gripped the Northern Plains, deflating prices and driving farmers off the land. Ironically, it was the failed banks, some in which Millard had invested, that enabled him to survive the collapse. Employed by the South Dakota Department of Banking to distribute assets of insolvent banks, he was kept busy. The more banks were in dire straits, the more likely he would draw a paycheck. He would move in, squeeze what he could out of the delinquent borrowers, and divide what was left among depositors and creditors. But Millard knew that he could not count on bank failures forever. Better times would staunch the bankruptcies; worse times will eliminate the banks. He was mining a narrow vein.
>
> A frugal man, he often used the bankrupt banks' stationery for his personal correspondence, and the letterheads chronicled a trail of failures that led him in the spring of 1927 to western South Dakota to oversee the demise of the First State Bank of

Phillip, the Bank of Interior, the Cottonwood State Bank and the First State Bank of Quinn. (Shuler, 1989)

The previous quote is particularly interesting for several reasons. First, Ben is assigned to go to his new base at the First State Bank of Phillip, South Dakota. Second, he is also assigned to work with the four other banks, all of which were either within the Badlands or on the edge of the Badlands. For example, Philip, on old US Highway 14 on the north side of the Bad River, is only about four or five miles north of the eastern edge of the Badlands. Third, Cedar Pass Lodge, Ben's home with his wife, son Herb, daughter-in-law Dorothy, and longtime friend Emin Vitalis, fell within the boundaries of the land that would become Badlands National Park and was only three miles east of Interior, South Dakota. It would be impossible to pick any five banks or towns closer to the Badlands than these places.

Although Ben's first arrival in the Badlands is documented, when he first met Senator Peter Norbeck is still unclear. Obviously, the announcement of the wedding of Ruth Norbeck, the senator's daughter, to Ben's nephew, Albert Jennings, was the high point and solid beginning of a close relationship between the two men. Norbeck was two years older than Ben and, unfortunately, would pass away in 1936, twenty years before Ben died. Ranger Shuler has described in some detail how the betrothed couple met and the absolutely critical and positive significance of this event to the eventual inclusion of the Badlands in the US National Park System. In some ways, the wedding also brought into play a second member of the Millard family, Ben's sister, Clara Jennings (Albert's mother), who was also one of Ben's significant business partners. Clara's role is described later by the Shuler book. Here, due to the significance of the resulting relationship between these seven people, including Grandmother

Estella (usually referred to as Stella), several lines from the Shuler book about Ruth and Albert are included:

> When her family moved to Washington in the fall of 1921, Ruth Norbeck stayed behind to enroll in the Lutheran Seminary in Red Wing, Minnesota. By the summer of 1922 she had decided to attend the University of South Dakota, in Vermillion, the school her father had studied in briefly in the 1880s. . . . In one of her letters, however, she casually mentioned that she was tired, and her solicitous parents began to fret. When she asked them for permission to stay in Vermillion for the summer term, they decided that she needed rest more than the extra credits. They were willing though for her "to wait on tables etc." at the game lodge in Custer State Park, no doubt feeling that a change of scenery would do her good. The whole family loved Custer State Park and spent as much time as they could there each summer.

> Ruth made waiting on tables at the game lodge an annual affair, and upon completing her junior year in the spring of 1926, she headed once again for the Black Hills, as did lodge handyman Albert Jennings, World War I veteran who had survived a poison gas attack in France. He and Ruth meet as coworkers at the lodge. Unlike Ruth, Albert had just earned a degree from South Dakota State College at Brookings.

Before they were married in the lodge on September 4, 1926, Ruth promised her parents that after the wedding she would earn her degree, a promise she kept.

In any case, before leaving Ranger Shuler's book, there is another quote of particular importance in this chain of coincidences:

To reach the bank at Interior from his headquarters in Phillip, he [Ben] had to negotiate the perilously steep, rutted road down Cedar Pass. Hence he read with personal interest newspaper stories appearing at the time about the imminent establishment of a National Park in the Badlands. (Shuler, 1989, p. 26)

Ben likely drove from Huron to Philip, maybe in one of the cars he had from his auto supply store. That trip, in itself, back in 1927, given the types of cars then plus the condition of the highway, would have taken some time and may have been quite an adventure depending on the weather. In any case, the trip down the hill in the Badlands would have convinced Ben that improving the roads to facilitate trips by tourists and even providing roads through the Badlands was a critical issue. Difficult driving conditions on the hill at Cedar Pass resulted in some drivers finding that the only way up the pass was to back up the hill in reverse gear, as there wasn't sufficient weight over the rear tires to go forward, especially if the roads were damp or wet.

Newspaper stories coming out when Ben first saw the Badlands must have, as Shuler pointed out, sparked his interest, but this, too, is another of the many coincidences that lined his path.

So now, after Ben's first introduction to the Badlands in the spring of 1927, only some seven or eight months after the Jennings-Norbeck wedding, the pace of work to obtain national park status went into high gear for the next few years. Senator Norbeck led the way on the complicated political front but also made many trips to the Badlands with Ben taking on various local aspects (designing and surveying the road, investigating land ownership, searching for headquarter site, etc.).

For readers who may not be familiar with Senator Norbeck, his background, interests, accomplishments, and political philosophy are all essential to both the Ben Millard story and the Badlands story. The relationship between Norbeck and Ben was so important and critical for the journey to have the Badlands become a national monument that I believe the comments below are particularly necessary:

Norbeck was born in the portion of the Dakota Territory that would later became the state of South Dakota. He is best remembered as "Mount Rushmore's great political patron" for promoting the construction of the giant sculpture at Mount Rushmore and securing federal funding for it. Norbeck was the oldest of six children born to immigrant [his father was Swedish and his mother Norwegian]. . . . At the time of Norbeck's birth, his family was living in a dugout on the family's 160 acres, located eight miles northeast of Vermillion, Dakota Territory. He attended . . . the University of South Dakota at Vermillion. In 1895 he was a contractor and driller of deep water, oil, and gas wells. He moved to Redfield, South Dakota in 1900 and added agricultural pursuits.

On May 9, 1908, Norbeck ran for the South Dakota State Senate from Spink County. After being elected to the first of three terms, he joined Coe Crawford's inner circle of Progressives. In 1914, Norbeck reluctantly accepted Governor Frank Byrne's invitation to run for Lieutenant Governor on the Republican ticket; they ended up winning.

In 1916, Norbeck ran for governor . . . becoming the ninth governor [and the first native-born governor] of South Dakota. He served in that office from 1917 to 1921. In

1920, Norbeck was elected United States Senator. He won the election with 50% of the vote. (Peter Norbeck, n.d.)

As a US senator, he was involved in sharing South Dakota with the rest of the country:

> Norbeck made a number of contributions to South Dakota's tourism industry. . . . He encouraged the development of the Iron Mountain Road in the Black Hills. He also pushed for the development of Sylvan Lake, Needles Highway, Badlands National Park, Custer State Park, Wind Cave National Park, and the Game Sanctuary in the Black Hills. (Peter Norbeck, n.d.)

The small but thorough book, *The History of Badlands National Monument and the White River Badlands,* is another reference pointing out additional interests, programs, and accomplishments of Senator Norbeck as well as his particular focus on gaining national park protection status for the Badlands, recognizing that the national monument designation would be a milepost on the way to protection as a national park. The following historical petitions will be referred to by Senator Norbeck in his replies to opposing factions in his intragovernmental battles at the federal level.

> Stimulated in part by various individuals and groups, the South Dakota legislature in 1909 petitioned the federal government to establish a township of Badlands as a national park. As read before both houses of Congress on March 16, 1909, the petition stated in part:

>> Whereas there is a small section of country about the headwaters of the White River in South Dakota where nature has carved the surface of the earth into most unique

and interesting forms, and has exposed to an extent perhaps not elsewhere found; and

Whereas this formation is so unique, picturesque, and valuable for the purpose of study that a portion of it should be retained in its native state.

However, no legislation was introduced on the proposal until more than a decade later.

A 1919 report by the U.S. Forest Service recommended that the Badlands area be set aside as a national park. The report also recorded considerable tourist travel to the Badlands. "The travel this year was several hundred times greater than in any former year . . ." Many visitors came over state route 40 (the Washington Highway) which connects the towns of Interior and Scenic with Rapid City. This road was under construction in 1919 and followed, more or less, the Chicago, Milwaukee and St. Paul railroad. Visitors also came on passenger trains. (Mattison & Grom, 1968, p. 27)

The same report recommended the road be built "along the course of the scenic points of interest" and that campground should be constructed "at well chosen camp sites." (Such a road was completed 16 years later by the State of South Dakota.)

While other individuals and organizations played an important part in the establishment of Badlands National Monument, Senator Peter Norbeck deserves more credit than any other legislator. . . . His achievements as governor were many, including the founding of a state-enterprise program designed to help farmers. Another of his great accomplishments with the establishment of Custer State Park.

Although his chief interest was in farm-relief legislation, he was instrumental in passing the Migratory Bird Act of 1929. (Mattison & Grom, 1968, pp. 27-28)

A final, very current reference on Senator Norbeck has some valuable and pertinent observations. For the 148th anniversary of the senator's birth, the *Daily Republic* paper published a colored insert on August 27th, 2018. On that day,

> Governor Dennis Daugaard [of South Dakota] signed off on a bill that proclaims Aug. 27 as the official Peter Norbeck holiday. State Rep. Julie Bartling presented the bill to a room full of proud Geddes community members honoring the late Norbeck.

> Peter Norbeck's long list of influential contributions to the state of South Dakota were celebrated Saturday in the small town where it all started for the first native-born governor. . . . It was only fitting to dedicate the Norbeck holiday on the day of the three-term U.S. senator's birth in the town that raised him to become a pioneer in the nation's first Progressive Movement which started gaining traction in the early 1900s. "He was influential in creating national landmarks such as Mount Rushmore and Grand Tetons National Park," [State Rep.] Bartling said. "Norbeck also invited former President Calvin Coolidge to visit the State Game Lodge in the Black Hills, where Coolidge later made the lodge his summer home."

> A lover of nature, Norbeck sponsored the Migratory Bird Treaty Act of 1918 and spearheaded efforts to construct bridges across the Missouri River during his time in the governor's chair from 1917 to 1921. . . . "Among the long list of accomplishments

Norbeck brought to South Dakota, he helped promote the beauty of our great state," Bartling said.

He developed a state highway program, a rural credit program and made monumental contributions to workmen's compensation laws and women's rights as governor.

An avid outdoorsman, Norbeck established the first ring-necked pheasant hunting season in the state, something Bartling sees as a living legacy, given the popularity of the sport. "Norbeck was a part of the first official pheasant hunt in the state in Spink County, and he was a truly pioneer for our state," Bartling said.

Brad Tennant, a history professor at Presentation College in Aberdeen, praised the contributions that Norbeck brought not only to the state, but to the country. Tennant was a guest speaker at a legislative session on August 27, 2018 at which the official Peter Norbeck holiday was created. In this speech he expressed how Norbeck was a leader for progressivism during the 1900s, prioritizing the general American public rather than specific groups. Norbeck was not against capitalism, but stood against unreasonable profit.

"During Norbeck's period of time in office, banks would be more than willing to give out loans at very high interest rates, and grain elevator operations would also take advantage of farmers by marking their profits down. This is what he saw as unfair and fought against," Tennant said. "That was also the spirit of the Progressive Movement."

Former U.S. President Theodore Roosevelt was a political figure whom Norbeck admired greatly. Roosevelt created five national parks in the U.S. during his time in office, which Norbeck paralleled at the state level during his time as governor when he created Custer State Park in the Black Hills. "Norbeck even referred to himself as a Roosevelt Republican," Tenant said.

Norbeck helped pave the way for women's rights and equality, which led to women being able to work and eventually vote. "He was one of the first governors in the country to address women's suffrage, and look at how much that progression has advanced today [2018]," Tenant said.

A Progressive Republican in a rural state wasn't exactly a common theme in the early 20th century, but Norbeck was one of four during that period of time to be considered a progressive Republican

"Norbeck as governor was certainly one of the leading progressive governors in the entire country," Tenant said. (Fosness, 2018)

Thinking about the trek Ben and Norbeck took to shepherd the Badlands toward national protection within the National Park System, it is difficult not to keep reflecting on the situation in the United States today. The current administration in Washington seems determined to do whatever it can to break down the barriers set up to protect scenic and historical areas such as the Bears Ears National Monument in southeastern Utah and the Boundary Waters Canoe Areas Wilderness in the Superior National Forest of Minnesota. The spirit of these attacks on our national parks is diametrically opposed to the philosophies and actions of two progressive Republicans—Senator Norbeck and Ben Millard.

Another pertinent example of actions taking place now concern fracking. Forces such as the powerful oil lobby are directing their efforts at eliminating protections of critical habitat grounds necessary for endangered species, such as the sage hen, to survive in western states. In many cases, these areas are already in use for private or public purposes as they have been for decades. Legions of cattle also graze on many of the federal and private lands in question. The protections afforded do not alter the land usage but seek to control vast changes in areas determined as critical for habitat protections. However, money and large corporate interests visualize the green dollar bills available if they could drill for oil; dig for copper, nickel, or uranium; or maybe just dig for sand for oil well cracking. The likelihood of polluting waters downstream in some areas has been determined to be too high a risk, and the resulting conditions would be left as a memento of our generation for later generations to deal with.

Grandfather's philosophy was definitely that of a conservative, small-town banker. His family members were mostly conservatives also, as were my mother, father, and Uncle Herb. To them, however, conservatism meant "conserving" and protecting some resources and figuring out other ways to "make do" as I often heard them say. Where are the conservative Republicans now—that I know are out there—and when are they going to speak up?

Another question I have is not political or divisive but a curiosity in a different vein. One of the best and most reliable sources of reference on my grandfather is the memorial brochure written in his honor by top management of the National Reserve Life Insurance Company. At the time of writing the memorial, the chairman of the board of directors and the president of the company made this observation:

> As Dean Member of the Board of National Reserve Life Insurance Company, Ben Millard's advice, counsel and ability was always recognized and appreciated. As in all his activities, he revealed his honest, upstanding character and reputation for fair dealing. (National Reserve Life Insurance Company, 1956)

The relationship I heard and saw between Grandfather and the National Reserve top officers was close. Therefore, the observations of the top National Reserve's officers on the relationship between Ben and Senator Norbeck are well grounded. The National Reserve's management group wrote that, "Senator Norbeck and Ben Millard had been close friends for many years" (1956).

Another observation was also made in the memorial brochure:

> During this time in the 20s while on a bank assignment at Phillip, South Dakota, near the big White River Badlands area, Ben Millard began to make frequent journeys around the region. The mysterious, gaunt and rugged beauty of this area appealed greatly to Ben Millard and he began to be imbued with the feeling that here in this historic and scenic region he wanted to spend the rest of his days. By an interesting coincidence, the late US Senator Norbeck of South Dakota, at this time was equally interested in the Black Hills area and was making plans to get it developed as a tourist attraction, which he felt positive would hold interest and appeal to millions of Americans. (National Reserve Life Insurance Company, 1956)

The curious and somewhat perplexing question that I have is whether or not grandfather and Norbeck had in fact been friends for a number of years prior to the Jennings-Norbeck wedding. On one hand, a well-written and documented reference mentioned earlier that is used for many of the significant aspects of Ben's Badlands story—*A Revelation Called the Badlands: Building a National Park, 1909–1939,* written by senior Badlands Park Ranger Shuler—described the Albert Jennings wedding of September 4th, 1926, like this: "Their wedding marked more than just the beginning of a marriage; it inaugurated a friendship that would play a pivotal role in the establishment of Badlands National Park" (1989). On the other hand, the Memorial Brochure states they had been friends for several years without mentioning the Jennings and Norbeck wedding.

The difference in emphasis between these two accounts may be a minor point, but it leads to the assumption that Senator Norbeck and Ben had met before the September wedding or at least had known and heard of each other earlier. My conclusion is that they had known each other for many years because, less than a year after the September wedding, Ben reported to Norbeck that his agenda was to be in the Badlands at the State Bank of Interior. Within another four or five months, Senator Norbeck and Ben would meet in person in the Badlands. Their agreed purpose was to survey and examine sites suitable for a hotel and cabins within the proposed park boundaries. The prompt establishment of an actual structure was an absolute necessity, and they both agreed it was important to be first on site and establish a physical footprint for a national park tourist facility.

That task was a highly complicated project involving all sorts of "publics" not the least of which were the political figures involved in Washington (mostly, of course, corralled and deftly managed by Senator Norbeck). At the same time, though, there were frequent visits by local officials who needed to see the place for themselves and assess the potentials of various angles being considered. Accordingly, a major part of Ben's job was convincing state and federal government visitors of the nature of the Badlands' uniqueness as a somewhat fragile geological and historical resource that deserved protection. In addition, he focused on the question of who should own this park, monument, or facility. Senator Norbeck and Ben were consistently and firmly convinced, as evidenced by their actions and foresight, that the owners of the Badlands should be the average US public and their guests. Without getting mired down into legalese, they saw their job as opening the monuments and parks to everyone, not just certain select groups, (this of course carries some ramifications regarding entrance and usage pricing,) and, for the average person, that meant the roads must show off the Badlands' best views. The knotty job was allowing visitors to be able to see the best views while also providing reasonable protection for the area.

Another large and diverse group made up of ranchers, multiuse visitors, campers, and so on, required Ben and Norbeck to be understanding, empathetic, reasonable, and skilled at listening and consensus building, as they shepherded the Badlands along its trail to protection.

All these interested groups voicing their needs and wishes made the placement of the road through the park, for example, a complicated endeavor.

Ben's and Senator Norbeck's mutual philosophy matched the philosophy and spirit of the Progressive movement. They felt an absolute necessity to do all they could to see the Badlands protected for future generations with a vision that turned out to be a partial road map of the National Park System.

Chapter 7: Surveying the Road, Cedar Pass, Pinnacles and My First Visit

At first glance, building a scenic road through the Badlands might seem easy enough to complete; after all, the process seems straightforward. However, several components must come together before a scenic road can be completed. The construction piece should be simple enough using the advanced mechanical road-construction equipment that was available, even during the last years of the 1920s and into the first years of the 1930s. The surveying and mapping part was more nuanced and tricky, requiring imagination and sense of purpose. The element of construction that vexes the planners and plagues the whole process of building from start to finish is the human relations part. That element includes many aspirations and ideals dividing the various groups involved. Just a few of these differences included local and national political differences, honest differences in the calculations of cost and maintenance, and differences of opinion about the importance of displaying the natural beauty of the surrounding scenery to the traveling public. All of these elements were vastly more difficult and frustrating to Norbeck and Ben, not only in the roadbuilding, but in the whole process of shepherding the Badlands into a national park designation for protection. Therein lies an educational story in the creation of a national park that deserves attention.

Once again, Ranger Shuler's book shows the interactions among the team members involved in the process of the Badlands becoming first a national monument and then a national park. Success in such an endeavor requires the team to demonstrate determination, resilience, compromise, and mutual support. In that vein, Ranger Shuler recorded a significant happening at the time:

By undertaking to push the Badlands bill through Congress during the hectic year of 1928, Peter Norbeck loaded his already heavy schedule to the breaking point. Most of the time he was compelled to stay in Washington, though he needed also to be in the Badlands collecting information about landownership in building the road.

Ben Millard was the solution to this problem. Norbeck's correspondence with him began in January of that year. Their first letters were businesslike dealing mostly with Millard's efforts to obtain leases from the Department of the Interior for his tourist operation. But in his very first letter, Millard commented about the lack of enthusiasm of a certain South Dakota highway engineer surveying the road through the park, and by the end of the summer their relationship had matured enough for them to share confidential political frustrations.

In Washington, Norbeck had to struggle over the Badlands with the Park Service in the Budget Office of the Department of the Interior, while back in South Dakota the powerful Rapid City Commercial Club vexed him every bit as much, exerting its influence in Pierre, it temporarily blocked the Badlands highway building program. (Shuler, 1989, p. 27)

Senator Norbeck believed that the Rapid City Commercial Club members might feel such a road through the Badlands would not, then, terminate in Rapid City. It is difficult to figure out their reasoning for this objection, but it may have been because they thought the new road might go around the city and directly to the Black Hills. Shuler goes on to point out, "Even local people on whom Norbeck had accounted for backing did not cooperate. Letters to them requesting information failed to bring any response" (1989, p. 27).

Particularly interesting about this situation is that if anyone had made huge contributions to Rapid City, South Dakota, it was Peter Norbeck, including all his work on development of the well-known Needles Highway and the entrance to Custer State Park thirty miles from Rapid City. The construction of that road is best described in a blurb on the Rapid City website:

> Deemed "impossible" to construct by its critics, Needles Highway (SD Hwy 87)—a National Scenic Byway—was completed in 1922. The road lies within the 71,000 acre Custer State Park, just 30 miles south of Rapid City, and is an impressive 14 mile stretch that includes sharp turns, narrow tunnels, granite spires, and world-class views. (The Impossible Highway, n.d.)

That stretch of road is now called the Peter Norbeck Scenic Byway.

Besides which, carving a road out of granite spires must have made the prospect of constructing the Loop Road in the Badlands look like child's play, especially when considering measuring to scale and then carving the mostly granite and quartz monzonite rock types of Mount Rushmore, which took fourteen years from 1927 to 1941 to construct. Senator Norbeck was the principal reason, due in part to his close relationship with President Coolidge, that federal funds were allocated for the planning and construction of Mount Rushmore.

Beyond that, Norbeck was responsible not only for the State Game Lodge, but also for the inclusion of a variety of animals and birds in the State Game Reserve surrounding the lodge.

Rapid City folks had very short memories at the time, particularly because Senator Norbeck had a vision and political philosophy aimed at protecting national resources for the enjoyment of the entire population, not just certain upper classes. Finally, he kept his focus on preserving the beauty of the natural surroundings and of planning roads and tourist facilities that allowed the general public to see the gorgeous gifts of nature that South Dakota has to offer.

A couple of quotes from letters between Senator Norbeck and Ben, as found in the research that Ranger Shuler did in Vermillion among Senator Norbeck's papers, specifically show that both men had the same vision for development of the Badlands as a national park. Obviously, Senator Norbeck had demonstrated his philosophy in all the fine work done in the Black Hills:

Millard agreed with Norbeck that his opponents were shortsighted and assured him that the Badlands road could be "a close second in wondrous beauty" to the scenic Norbeck-designed Needles Highway in the Black Hills. He [Ben Millard] offered to collaborate with him "in making the new highway show these lands to the very best advantage," attracting "thousands upon thousands of people from all over the United States to South Dakota."

Naturally enough, the South Dakota Highway Department, which was obligated to build the road, was trying to keep costs low. Avoiding the rugged country along the Badlands Wall, their engineers routed the Badlands Loop Road north from the Pinnacles and then east through 15 miles of gentle prairie all the way to Bigfoot Pass. This meant that more than half of the road would miss Badlands scenery entirely, passing instead through cattle-grazed grasslands. Communities like Quinn favored this route. It would detour tourist traffic almost to their doors.

Millard, however, objected when he saw what the engineers had done. They had missed the vital point that scenery was the reason for the existence of the road, and he set out to remedy their lack of esthetic insight. He carefully explored the steep tortured slopes southeast of the Pinnacles and discovered a practical route down into the rugged, brilliantly colored Yellow Mounds Area. From thence, traveling east, he headed up through Dillon Pass and into the prairie close to the Wall—skimming the edge in places—to Bigfoot Pass. Building along this route would cost more than the one the engineers laid out, but it would show off the best scenery the Badlands had to offer. Ultimately, Millard and Norbeck extended the road east from Bigfoot Pass close to the Wall and up through Cedar Pass, in all twenty-seven miles of magnificent views blending one into another. (1989, pp. 28-29)

In addition to the problems with the local Rapid City folks, other communities, such as Quinn, were also disappointed by the layout of the Loop Road. Probably the hardest hit town by the new Loop Road layout was Interior. For example, currently, still some ninety years later, strong feelings of opposition to the road that was laid out by Ben and approved by Norbeck remain in the town.

Because Ben and Senator Norbeck insisted that the Loop Road must be designed to show off as much of the best of the Badlands as possible, the decision was made to have Highway 240, the Loop Road, turn northwest just past what is now the Ben Reifel Visitor Center, the Badlands

National Park Headquarters, and the Cedar Pass Lodge complex, leaving the junction with State Highway 44, which continues on to the three towns of Interior, Scenic, and Rapid City.

This road design was chosen because after just a couple of hundred yards, westbound Highway 44 leaves the Badlands formations and enters flat prairie en route to Interior and beyond, whereas the Badlands Wall formations trend northwesterly. Earlier, in fact, to construct the designed Loop Road, the engineers and road builders had to carve out the first tunnel to gain access to the first parts and contiguous Badlands Wall formations that run unabated up to the Pinnacles. The northwestern termination of the Badlands Loop Road is a few miles south of the community of Wall, South Dakota. As a result, when the road was finally completed in 1935, traffic on Highway 44 through Interior dwindled to a trickle. Obviously, various businesses, definitely including the motel, were badly hit. The town of Interior was and still is an active but very small town. Located just three miles west of Cedar Pass Lodge on Highway 44, it lies just outside the boundary of the park by about a mile and a half. Highway 44 continues thirty-two miles west through Interior and then on to Rapid City.

Interior is still the closest post office to Cedar Pass Lodge, and there used to be a small but well-stocked hardware store owned and ran by Joe and Mabel Haight. Back in the mid-1940s they had one of the few party line telephones we could use (as mentioned earlier). Interior also had a grocery store, a liquor store, and one or two bars that served food (one still does and is well thought of locally). Other businesses and organizations, such as a gas station, limited auto repairs, churches, and a well-frequented motel, were critical supports for Cedar Pass Lodge as the larger towns required longer travel, and weather could present serious problems.

For many years, Interior was also the regular stop of the Milwaukee Railroad line from Mitchell, South Dakota, in the East River country. The Milwaukee line crosses the Missouri River at Chamberlain, South Dakota, which remains a relatively large town, and continues west through the last somewhat sizable town of Kadoka, South Dakota, thirty miles east of the Badlands. "The new townsite of Kadoka was one of many that quickly sprang up following the 1907 construction of the Milwaukee's new Rapid City Line" (Renewable Technologies, 2007, p. 20).

These towns were vital as service providers for places such as Cedar Pass Lodge. For example, Grandfather and Uncle Herb insisted that Cedar Pass Lodge's dining room and kitchen must offer a well-thought-out, home-cooked family menu every day. Such a menu had to include all home-cooked and prepared main courses of meat and vegetables plus fresh salads served in a proper manner but at reasonable prices. Of course, as Grandfather was well aware from having raised a family of three kids and from his experiences in Ruskin Park, a good selection of ice cream and homemade desserts was equally important. The word about the reasonably priced high-quality food got around quickly and as far away as Chicago.

According to Ranger Shuler's research, in 1922, only a year after first arriving in Washington as a newly elected senator, Norbeck wrote his first bill to establish a National Park of the Badlands. Submitting that bill was Norbeck's first introduction to politics in Washington as he learned the difference between introducing a bill and having it voted on and approved. When the bill was reintroduced in the House of Representatives in 1923, it died again; however:

> In August of 1923, Norbeck wrote the Commissioner of the General Land Office in Washington seeking information about homesteads in the Badlands. He wanted the

data he explained because he intended "to make a serious effort to have the whole Badlands area set aside as a National Monument or National Park." It took a while, but by the fall of 1927, his continuing efforts to create the Badlands park was making progress in Washington and was well publicized throughout South Dakota. (Shuler, 1989, pp. 17-18)

Again, I marvel at how curious it is that these coincidences keep lining up for my grandfather. As I wrote in Chapter 6, Grandfather was regularly driving down the rutted road of the ridge soon to bear his name—Millard Ridge—and passing by the future location of his new home, Cedar Pass Lodge, to the Bank of Interior on his first assignment. He was exposed to the newspaper reporting on the possibility of the Badlands being considered for national park designation as Ranger Shuler noted the discussions going on regarding that possibility.

Ranger Shuler pointed out that the letter to the commissioner had let the cat out of the bag concerning talks on a possible Badlands National Park. Almost immediately, other communities and people also got into the act. All that interest of others prompted Ben and Senator Norbeck to conclude that they better get going on the plan formulated by Grandfather and his business partner and sister, Clara Jennings, of establishing a physical presence before someone else or some other organization took up the idea. If they had a chance to use their combined and agreed visions and experience of how to create and protect an area such as the Badlands for future generations, as so amply demonstrated by Senator Norbeck in the Black Hills, they had to get started promptly.

The steps taken by Norbeck to lay the first virtual brick on the trail with that letter to the commissioner are carefully outlined by Ranger Shuler:

> Harriet De Hahn, one of two sisters who ran the general store at Conata [SD], heard that a Badlands Highway might be built and wanted it routed through Conata. The owner of Palmers Drug Store in Interior urged that the new road pass through Interior. Pressured by Norbeck, the South Dakota Highway Department surveyed the road through Cedar Pass. James Bateman, Commissioner of Jackson County at the east end of the proposed park, looked over the route. "It sure looks good," he wrote the senator.
>
> Needing an official Park Service record on the Badlands in order to proceed, Norbeck put the Secretary of the Interior on notice on November 2nd that the South Dakota congressional delegation was ready to try again to pass a "Badlands National Park Bill." (Shuler, 1989, p. 18)

At this point, politics and turf protection really come into full play, and the story becomes an example of how difficult it is to get national park designation through the morass. Once again, it's shocking to consider how quickly people forgot Senator Norbeck's past efforts and successes in trying to protect natural places for future generations to enjoy.

As stated earlier, Senator Norbeck and Ben agreed that they wanted a national park in the Badlands as soon as possible, as evidenced here:

> Early in the fall of 1927, they explored the Badlands together to locate sites for Millard and his sister to lease from the federal government for a refreshment stand, a hotel and a camp. They agreed that a refreshment stand would do well at the Pinnacles, a high

point with a wonderful view nine miles south of Wall [SD]. For the campground and hotel, they favored a site in the Juniper Grove at Cedar Pass.

Norbeck advised Millard to apply for leases at the Land Department at Pierre and if turned down, take up the matter with the General Land Office in Washington, D.C. His applications were rejected in January 1928. Millard had been blocked by Norbeck's own regulation—the 1922 executive order withdrawing federal lands in the Badlands from public occupation. (Shuler, 1989, p. 6)

In substance, Grandfather and his sister were running into a brick wall of refusals, but they continued to feel they must get started right away in building a structure. To that end,

Clara Jennings, purchased a tract of private land at $10 an acre on the relatively flat prairie at the foot of Cedar Pass, and she and her brother began to build on it. They regarded this site as temporary, to serve only until the more scenic location in the Cedar Grove could be acquired.

Careful planning was essential, and in this Millard's experience in developing a resort in Eastern South Dakota [Ruskin Park] was invaluable. It was uncertain whether existing traffic into the Badlands could sustain a hotel there. Building a profitable business might take time. (Shuler, 1989, p. 26)

At this juncture, Ben's proven management and marketing skills, which had been demonstrated in the major Ruskin Park venture, came into play. As recounted in Chapter 4, he had successfully run the park for several years as the active day-to-day manager and marketing agent.

The odds of a successful business in the Badlands, based on Ben's experience in Ruskin Park, would have appeared highly likely. But that's with hindsight and his record of success in Ruskin Park. When Ben and Dowdell bought Ruskin Park in 1809, the park already had a huge, established clientele. In addition, the previous owners had constructed a small train depot and thousands of people came directly to the park by train. Mitchell, South Dakota's sixth largest city, was only twenty-five miles away. Home of the famous Corn Palace, Mitchell was a renowned convention center and tourist destination. What Ben didn't know, at the time of building a hotel, cabins, and dance hall in the Badlands in 1928, was whether there as any chance of drawing enough traffic to support a business.

Ben had shown earlier that after he had carefully considered opportunities versus costs in many projects, he was willing to bet the farm, if necessary, on the project in which he was interested. The Badlands had definitely captured his interest, and he was planning to live there for the rest of his days and work on protecting the Badlands with Senator Norbeck. So, as Ranger Shuler discovered, he went "whole hog" into the building and marketing at Cedar Pass:

> Millard temporized by constructing a dance hall from inexpensive bark-covered board slabs trucked from Black Hills lumber mills and within weeks a rustic but stylish pavilion took shape. Millard engaged bands to play at the pavilion once or twice a week and on holidays and mounted an $800 advertising blitz that brought in customers from as far as Rapid City, almost 90 miles to the west. A cabin maid, Ilo Nelson remembered both the Virginia Ravens, a black band, and a band led by Lawrence Welk, who had not yet discovered "Champagne Music." At this stage of Welk's career, his bands went by names like the Hotsy Totsy Boys and the Honolulu Fruit Gum Orchestra.

The imposing building had a kitchen, a counter for curios, cigars and candy, and the dining room, the moneymaker. Several small metal cabins were constructed for tourists who would eventually become the foundation of the business. Millard gave his dance hall the unlikely name, Cedar Pass Hotel. It was doing a brisk business on the evening of July 28, when [US] Senator Nye's subcommittee stopped by for dinner. The assembled officials could hardly fail to notice that Millard was operating an efficient and attractive tourist business, improving chances that eventually Millard would get his Badlands leases. (Shuler, 1989, p. 26)

Although not much official information is available on whether the leases at the Pinnacles came through or not, I know firsthand that they did.

In the fall of 1935, my dad had told us that we ought to try to make a trip to the Badlands next year because the new Badlands Loop Road had been completed. The date was set for the end of Spring classes. In May of 1936, we began our first extended automobile trip to the Badlands with Mother and Father in our father's Chrysler Airflow. Glenna and I were pretty excited, to say the least; it was a big deal for the two of us.

We pretty much followed the route Grandfather had taken as a child, though we didn't take the swing down to Nebraska and Decatur where he had worked on a riverboat. We did get to see Crystal Lake, Minnesota, where Grandfather was born on a nearby farm, and we also got to check out where Dad was born in Canton, South Dakota, just outside of Sioux Falls. However, by then, even though we were riding in the lap of luxury in what was then a space-age-looking vehicle, Glenna and I were getting pretty antsy to see the Badlands. A couple times, though, when there were straight, unencumbered highway stretches where we could see what seemed like ten miles in any direction, my dad would put the pedal to the metal and try out the Airflow. Glenna and I were pretty impressed, but Mother put a damper on that. We knew she was a better driver than Dad anyway.

I recall much of that road trip. I most definitely remember how the landscape changed after we crossed the Missouri River at Chamberlain and entered into the West River country of South Dakota, leaving the East River country, behind. Glenna and I were impressed with the ice cream cones we got in Artesian, South Dakota, where Dad had gone to grade school and Grandfather had his office in the bank he had owned.

The drive was long, about 500 miles, so we stayed overnight somewhere. I think it was in Mitchell, South Dakota, because I remember seeing the Corn Palace, which I've gone back to see a couple times. Mitchell is a busy town now, right on Interstate 90. We drove to Philip, South Dakota, and south to Cedar Pass to stay overnight and visit with Grandfather. The next morning, we took the new Loop Road, which was pretty amazing, but we were sure ready to get out of the car and see Grandmother ("Neno," as most of her grandchildren called her) and Uncle Herb. Grandmother worked at the Pinnacles many of the summers in those days as it was a significant operation.

View southwest from Millard Ridge of the Cedar Pass Lodge
and cabins with the White River in the background.

Parts of my first trip to the Badlands are perfectly clear in my head, but I don't recall much

about Cedar Pass Lodge. However, I do recall a great deal about our stay at the Pinnacles gift

shop and sleeping quarters, where Uncle Herb and Grandmother were there as our hosts.[14]

Grandfather always used to tell tourists in his presentations that although the day might be

very hot, they were going to need a blanket at night. The Pinnacles are one of the highest spots

in the Badlands, and it cools off after the sun goes down even more than it does at Cedar Path

Lodge, which is much lower. By early morning, we often needed a sweater.

As a result, in the morning on the 1936 trip, when my sister and I got up as Uncle Herb called

out that he was about ready to start preparing breakfast, he appeared wearing his red long

---

[14] I can still recall watching my father when he was a few years older than I am now. Occasionally, some event or site would trigger a memory. His eyes seemed transfixed in an odd, long, far-reaching gaze. When the ancient specter or sound released him from his trance, he would say that he had just recalled some experience back when he was a young kid. The memory was so clear that it was frightening to him and that it seemed as if it just happened yesterday.
Similarly, as I have been in the process of researching and writing this book, certain letters or photographs will now trigger my memories of that trip over eighty years ago. Especially clear are the memories of Grandmother and Uncle Herb at the Pinnacles location where we stayed for a few days.

underwear. I had never seen red long underwear nor had my sister. We thought it was one of the funniest things we'd ever seen, and we kept kidding Uncle Herb about it.

The Pinnacles building was a long, rectangular, fairly narrow building as I remember it, with lots of windows to see the incredible view from up high on the small plateau. Air conditioning apparatuses were scarce in those days, and fans—large and small—and exhaust vents were the principal sources of cooling. But likely, Uncle Herb had installed a "swamp cooler" near the ice cream cooler. At six and seven years old, I know that Glenna and I felt like we had died and gone to heaven. There were so many cool things to look at, and we spent much of the two or three days we were there in the store. Neno spoiled us rotten with ice cream and cookies.

Concerning the operations in the store at the Pinnacles and also at Cedar Pass Lodge, the goods sold were of high quality. Uncle Herb was the forager, buyer, and store manager at both locations. He became well known for his excellent work at Cedar Pass Lodge. Suffice it to say that the income from the Pinnacles, which was a low-overhead and low-cost operation, was substantial and necessary for the future improvements at Cedar Pass Lodge to carry it through very tough days during World War II when tourist traffic dwindled to almost nothing, and Uncle Herb had volunteered for service in the US Navy, leaving Grandmother, Grandfather, and Emin Vitalis to run the place with the help of a few extremely loyal staff members. I know from copies of letters from our family files that Grandmother was near the breaking point due to the difficulties and strain.

The other picture of the trip that is still vivid on the front page of my memory is of a big fossil Uncle Herb had found and kept in a case near one of the counters. In addition to that, he had all sorts of agates and minerals. I recall that those agates looked to me then like Minnesota Lake Superior agates that I was familiar with. His agates, which he had polished himself, had gorgeous stripes in them. He also had, in my young mind, a bewildering collection of minerals, fossils, and petrified wood. Near the Badlands, there are thousands of acres of stone fields where avid hunters, known as "rock-hounds," from all over the United States and other countries spend hours and days enjoying this pastime.

Herbert Millard's lapidary sale display area at the Cedar Pass Lodge, 1948.

Now, I know that the agates that impressed me so much must have been the famous Fairburn agates of South Dakota, later elevated to the designation of the South Dakota State Gem. Uncle Herb had quite a few of them. When this story moves on to the mid-1940s after Uncle Herb returned from serving in the US Navy as a gunnery officer, he often took me on agate and mineral hunting field trips in the Buffalo Gap National Grassland near the Badlands National Park. Uncle Herb had a penchant for digging into a subject and keeping at it until he could intelligently discuss it with anyone. South Dakota and the Badlands was the perfect place for his interests in geology and lapidary pursuits. At Cedar Pass Lodge, he established a substantial lapidary shop, showroom, and retail shop downstairs in the old dining room. It was a classy looking facility with the cedar wood walls and good lighting. Lucky for me, he told Aunt Dorothy before he passed away that he wanted me to have his agate collection, of which I did receive a portion that included some really nice Fairburn agates, polished and marked with IDs.[15]

The quantity and quality of the minerals and stones adjacent to the Badlands is so high that one of the principal points in South Dakota's marketing efforts to attract visitors is their lapidary and minerals, as well as fossils and petrified wood deposits in the Buffalo Gap Grasslands.[16]

---

[15] As one of my lifelong hobbies has been looking for agates beginning even before my first trip to the Badlands, I became really hooked on that hobby beginning eighty-plus years ago, in the days I am now writing about.

[16] The National Park Service provides good, free information about what to see and look for in nearby areas, outside of the boundaries of the National Badlands Park, and in adjacent areas, such as the Buffalo National Grasslands, where it is also free for rock hounds to search for agates, fossils, or minerals.

Chapter 8: The Depression Years – Ben Millard Buys and Donates Land for the Badlands National Monument

The phrase "Depression years" can conjure up two distinct pictures based on a viewer's background and knowledge of history—depression of the pocketbook or depression of the mind (or maybe both).

For more than a decade, landowners had been facing both depression of the pocketbook *and* depression of the mind as they watched the value of their ranch or farmland fall until the property value was less than the money owed on the land. On top of that, news of further impending catastrophes of grasshopper plagues, drought, and Dust Bowl winds were in local and regional news and discussed by neighbors.

The situation facing Ben and his new Badland's pursuit was complex. He was deeply involved in the acquisition of land or for a proposed national monument or national park. At the same time, he was working at stabilizing the local banking system with restructuring, if possible, or foreclosure, if necessary, of small-town banks.

On the other side of the land acquisition process, Ben was looking at land prices that were the lowest in his memory. He needed to buy lands as quickly as possible to meet requirements set by politicians before they would move the Badlands to protected status.

At this juncture in his job, Ben's background as a banker, real estate owner, and businessman made him the right man, in the right place, at exactly the right time to complete the land purchasing tasks set out for him by Senator Norbeck. Ben had the empathy and understanding to negotiate with the suffering and depressed landowners.

The National Park Service (NPS) book, *The History of the Badlands National Monument*,[17] described Ben's work this way:

> Among local persons who worked hard toward the establishment of Badlands National Monument after it was authorized in 1929 were Ben H. Millard, the original owner of Cedar Pass Lodge; A. G. Granger of Kadoka; Leonel Jensen, local rancher; Ted E. Hustead, owner and operator of the well-known Wall Drug Store; and Dr. G. W. Mills of Wall.
>
> Of these individuals, Mr. Millard made the greatest contribution to the establishment and development of the national monument.
>
> Millard worked closely with Senator Norbeck on development plans for the proposed Badlands National Monument. . . . (He) was responsible for federal acquisition of private lands, much of which later became a part of the national monument after it was established in 1939. (Mattison & Grom, 1968, p. 37)

Ranger Shuler's book details what happened in the final days of the Norbeck–Millard joint effort:

---

[17] This book is free on the web as an NPS publication at http://npshistory.com/publications/badl/history/.

Millard became Norbeck's alter ego in matters of the road and unscrambling the helter-skelter of private and government land. Dealing with land proved more intractable than designing the road. But Millard's experience in real estate and finance had prepared him for the task. His first contribution came towards the end of 1928 when pressures on the Senator were greatest to supply information to Congress and government agencies. Millard offered to draw up and send to him a map of the area detailing ownership.

Throughout, Millard devoted himself to the cause. He used his own money to buy options on land for sale when government funds were not available and later sold them to the state at no profit. Norbeck saw no problem with that, and the practice continued into 1934 when the pace of federal land buying in the Badlands suddenly accelerated. The Submarginal Land Division of the National Park Service had been established to help relieve the suffering brought on by the terrible drought, depression, and the deflated land prices. The Park Service bought up agricultural tracks on which it was no longer possible to make a living, but which were valuable for recreation. Most landowners welcomed the buyer, even the federal government. Many owed more in property taxes that the land was worth.

Norbeck was quick to apply the program to an extension of the authorized Badlands National Monument. In April 1934 he wired Millard to check current land prices and find out if a township—thirty-six square miles—could be added without arousing local opposition.

The rains had failed that spring. Grass was sparse and it appeared there would be no hay to carry cattle over the winter. Ranchers as far North of the Badlands as Philip drove their herds down to the Pine Ridge Indian Reservation where grazing was available. Millard did not have to conduct a survey to answer Norbeck's inquiry—land was cheap, owners were ready to sell.

After six years of volunteering, Millard suddenly found himself on a payroll. "I am now working for the National Park System in the purchasing of land of the Park Extension," he wrote Norbeck. His official title was Project Manager, with authority and money to negotiate options and accept offers to sell. By the summer of 1935, Millard had brought thousands of Badlands acres into federal ownership. (Shuler, 1989, pp. 29-30)

In writing his book, Shuler had access to Senator Norbeck's personal letters in Vermillion, South Dakota, at the university. Those letters could and did fill in the political morass that Ben was slugging through. A lot happened in that period of roughly a year and a half during which Senator Norbeck, in his declining days, must have felt deserted and watched sadly as hopes of seeing the Badlands protected appeared to be vanishing. For Ben's part, his long partnership with Senator Norbeck backfired on him as Senator Norbeck's health and political power faded.

However, by then, the seeds had been planted for an incipient problem for Ben that had been germinating during that single year of 1935 when working for the NPS.

Federal employment was a godsend for Millard. He believed in his job, which advanced the struggle to make a national park in the Badlands—he liked the work, and he needed the money. But no getting around it, he was serving three masters. He worked for and was paid by the National Park Service. He labored without pay, but with deep loyalty, for Senator Norbeck. And he managed his sister's tourist business at Cedar Pass. For all that, he genuinely loved the Badlands, and probably saw no conflict of interest between serving Norbeck, the National Park Service, and his sister. Surely, what was good for one was good for the others. He would be deeply offended if anyone suggested otherwise. (Shuler, 1989, p. 31)

Through a letter, Norbeck passed on that he had learned, in essence, that forces were out to get Ben. These disparaging NPS forces felt that Ben was hired to purchase land for the NPS but had refused to sell his Cedar Pass property. Norbeck told him that rumor also had it that Ben was holding on to some land for his own personal gain.

Norbeck advised Ben to try to clear up the misunderstanding as Norbeck did not believe any of the rumors. But the winds continued to feed the seeds planted. Ranger Shuler observed that probably the most severe problem was that it was obvious Ben and Norbeck were so close that Ben seemed to serve as Norbeck's eyes and ears.

Attempts on the part of both Senator Norbeck and Ben failed to resolve the misunderstandings. There were too just too many people that had strong feelings and were not in the mood to listen. The last straw was a letter written to the director of the NPS by Senator Norbeck, who, frustrated and worn down by his medical problems, was critical of the NPS's design and plan to implement a road from the Sage Creek Basin to the Sheep Mountain Area. Both Senator Norbeck and Ben objected on the same basis they had fought over on the Loop Road. They felt that, once again, the proposed road lacked adequate attention to the visual aspects.

Senator Norbeck's final days are left to the end of this chapter as there are significant aspects that need mentioning due to the vast changes that took place when the country's new president, Franklin D. Roosevelt, took office in March of 1933. He weighed in on the national monument proposal and on relief for the hundreds of thousands of farmers and ranchers suffering the effects of the Great Depression.

> The alphabet agencies (also New Deal agencies) were the U.S. federal government agencies created as part of the New Deal of President Franklin D. Roosevelt. The earliest agencies were created to combat the Great Depression in the United States and were established during Roosevelt's first 100 days in office in 1933. William Safire notes that the phrase "gave color to the charge of excessive bureaucracy." Democrat Al Smith, who turned against Roosevelt, said his government was "submerged in a bowl of alphabet soup."
>
> In total, at least 100 offices were created during Roosevelt's terms of office as part of the New Deal, and "even the Comptroller-General of the United States, who audits the government's accounts, declared he had never heard of some of them." (Alphabet Agencies, n.d.)

Interestingly enough, Ben was reported to have worked for one of those alphabet agencies. From 1969:

> Millard worked closely with Senator Norbeck on development plans for the proposed Badlands National Monument. From September 1934 through July 1936, he was

employed as a local Resettlement Administration [RA] project manager. (Mattison &

Grom, 1968, p. 37)

A little more about that agency follows:

The Resettlement Administration (RA) was a New Deal U.S. feral agency created May 1,

1935. It relocated struggling urban and rural families to communities planned by the

federal government. On September 1, 1937, it was succeeded by the Farm Security

Administration.

The RA was the brainchild of Rexford G. Tugwell, an economics professor

at Columbia University who became an advisor to Franklin D. Roosevelt . . . Roosevelt

established the RA under Executive Order 7027, as one of the New Deal's "alphabet

agencies" . . . After facing enormous criticism for his poor management of the RA,

Tugwell resigned in 1936. (Resettlement Adminstration, n.d.)

In 1933, the agricultural land crisis, which had begun in 1919, hit Ben's large real estate

operation back in the East River country of South Dakota, and much of his land was valued at less

than the taxes owed on it. Rancher Ben Zoss confirmed as much to me during our interview. He

had examined several tax records in the Sanborn County offices.

Also, in 1933, Franklin D. Roosevelt became president, having received approximately 57

percent of the vote and taking forty-two of the forty-eight states. As a result, it was very

apparent that the country was seeking some help from the various agencies. The farmers in the

South, Midwest, and particularly the Great Plains states, including South Dakota, had been hit or would shortly be hit by the three D's discussed earlier: the drought, the Depression, and the Dust Bowl.

If those conditions weren't enough, for farmers and ranchers within the planned boundaries of the proposed Badlands National Monument, many were probably keeping in touch with agricultural agencies about the locations and directions of travel of the clouds of grasshoppers decimating crops and fields.

It's clear that that the plains states can be a tough master for a farmer or rancher. If the growing season turns out to be good, the lure of the land can tempt those facing difficulties in the cities to think of moving. It is reasonable to assume that, some homesteaders, encouraged by the saying attributed to Horace Greely, of "Go West, young man," may have decided to follow the urging of Greely:

> [He] saw the fertile farmland of the West as an ideal place for people willing to work hard for the opportunity to succeed. The phrase came to symbolize the idea that agriculture could solve many of the nation's problems of poverty and unemployment characteristic of the big cities of the East. It is one of the most quoted sayings from the nineteenth century and may have had some influence on American history. (Go West, young man, n.d.)

Harsh winters brought another challenge to living and working on the Great Plains as ranchers had to protect their livestock should a fast-moving winter snowstorm and cold snap hit the area. I've heard several personal stories over the years from very close friends of Grandfather and Uncle Herb about the drastic effects of winter storms on nearby friends' cattle. For example, I was told by Keith Crew of a particularly fast moving and dangerous snowstorm that happened only a very few years ago. He and his son Grady were able to get all the cattle in, but

several of their neighbors were too late and lost almost their entire heard. Besides that, the

storm covered a wide area and was written up as breaking news.

Keith's parents Leslie and Jessie Crew were like part of the extended family when I was a kid.

They owned a ranch that borders the northeastern corner of the Badlands National Park. Keith,

who is a couple years my senior, still runs the ranch with his son and grandson. Keith took a

project under his wing of assembling information and making an inventory of the Prairie

Homestead, the sod house and barn of the Brown family, which was part of Leslie and Jessie's

ranch property. Due to Keith's unbounded energy and determination, the Prairie Homestead is

on the National Register of Historic Places and is open to the public to visit and see.

Neighbor Keith Crew at his ranch next to the Badlands with a Scottish Highlander breed of
cattle. 1956.

The Brown family farm contains the original furniture, clothing, and kitchenware, along with the

barn and root cellar. All Badlands visitors and their families should make a point to stop and visit the place, located right on the beginning of the Badlands Loop Road at the eastern end, on the last private property before entering the park.

> The Prairie Homestead is a sod house located at 21070 South Dadota Highway 240 north of Interior, South Dakota . The house was constructed by Ed Brown and his wife in 1909. The Browns built their home with sod bricks and topped it with a grass roof. Western South Dakota was one of the last regions of the state to be settled by homesteaders, and the house is now one of the few remaining sod homes in the state. (Prairie Homestead, n.d.)

American homesteaders who headed to the West faced daunting problems, which, in many cases, caused them to give up their dream, forfeit their land, and leave. The problem was bad enough for US citizens, but often advertisements run in foreign countries touting the incredible advantages of immigrating to the United States to adopt an agricultural homestead vastly and, really, immorally, exaggerated the advantages.

> A potential homesteader's first hurdle was to gather sufficient funds to travel west, build a suitable house, fence property, and purchase tools and seed. And a pioneer needed enough money to support himself until he made his land self-supporting.

> Once in a chosen area, the prospective homesteader was often confronted by the reality that the only available acreage was inferior farmland far from transportation. To get good land in the West, one had to buy from speculators and land jobbers, and the prices ranged often from 1 to 15 dollars an acre

The authors of the Homestead Act imagined that settlers would find well-watered acreage that would provide the wood for fuel, fences, and the construction of homes, as in the East. Homesteads on the tall grass prairie of Minnesota, Iowa, eastern Nebraska, and Kansas roughly met these expectations. But for those who settled further west, the land did not always offer readily available water and wood.

The homesteader's first task often was to build a house where there was no timber. Pioneers usually built a dugout first, scooping a hole in the side of [a] hill, blocking the front with a wall of cut sod, and covering the top with a few poles that held up a layer of prairie grass and dirt. These homes were often washed away by rains and were always dirty.

Still, they housed whole families for months or even years before giving way to a more permanent structure—the sod house.

The next task was to obtain water where no springs existed. If the frontiersman lived near a stream, he hauled water to his home in barrels; if not, he depended on collected rainwater. Others dug wells by hand. In lowlands near streams, wells were only 40 or 50 feet deep. On higher tablelands, water lay 200 or 300 feet below the surface. Not until the 1880s was well-drilling machinery commonly available to pioneer families.

Then came the task of keeping warm when there was little ready fuel. . . . Special stoves for burning hay were widely sold during the 1870s. The plains environment made life difficult and defeated the dreams of many.

Every season brought new hardships. Floods often surged across the countryside during the spring. Summer usually ushered in a wave of heat and drought. In hot temperatures, streams dried up, animals died, and work was made that much harder. (Bradsher, 2012, p. 32)

My first trip to the Badlands, as noted earlier, was in May of 1936. These were also the last few months of Senator Norbeck's life as he fought with cancer of the jaw. The senator died December 20th, 1936. As I read Park Ranger Shuler's description of Senator Norbeck's final days, a somewhat uncharacteristically despondent look at the future seemed evident:

That Norbeck's time ran out meant the end of any hope that the Badlands would become a national park rather than a national monument. No one else had the commitment to get the necessary park bill through Congress—it was much simpler to rely on Presidential proclamation already on track. (Shuler, 1989, p. 33)

Perhaps I'm being too sensitive, but I was surprised by Shuler's grim conclusion, especially with all the people Shuler mentioned so far as energized supporters of the effort to see the Badlands bill carried forward as well as the work they had already done. His conclusion appears to be at odds with the last few notes in his book. The book was published or presumably written after both the national monument and the national park status for the Badlands had been enacted. I feel I may have a better inference regarding Shuler's sentiment. After he had seen and outlined all the frustrations in the political morass in Washington and between agencies, he was commiserating with what Senator Norbeck must have felt.

And yet, on the final page of the book, Shuler wrote:

Perhaps, after all, Norbeck had done what he could before he died, and that the time had come for the bureaucracy to take over. A park service official in the Washington office noted in a handwritten memo of January 27th, 1937, that the Senator's death "will probably take the 'spotlight' off the project," and that "the Badlands plans are in much better shape now and being approved through all the regular channels."

In two years, all was in order. On January 25, 1939, the President of the United States of America signed the document containing these words:

NOW, THEREFORE, I, FRANKLIN D. ROOSEVELT, President of the United States of America . . . do proclaim that . . . the following-described lands in South Dakota are hereby set aside, dedicated, and reserved as the Badlands National Monument. (1989, p. 34)

Along with a full-length photo of Ben, Shuler wrote the following:

Ben Millard's low point, when he lost his job with the National Park Service, did not end his contributions to building a National Park in the Badlands. In 1937 he bought the Cedar Pass Lodge from his sister, Clara Jennings, and continued to manage it as he had since 1928, providing facilities which made it possible for visitors to spend as much time as they pleased in the monument. Always promoting the Badlands, Millard gave nightly geology lectures to his guests at Cedar Pass—thus he was the first Badlands interpreter. When the Park Service needed a site for a headquarters building and visitors' center, he donated 28 acres for that purpose. He never ceased the campaign for local support for the Park. His work paid off. Gradually visitors to the Badlands Monument increased in number, as did the guests of the Cedar Pass Lodge.

He was eighty-four-years-old when he died at the Cedar Pass Lodge on March 23, 1956.

On June 28, 1957, he was accorded a rare honor. Acknowledging his profound contributions to the Badlands National Monument, the National Park Service had a prominent section of the Wall about a mile northeast of the Cedar Pass Lodge officially named Millard Ridge. Steep and almost inaccessible, glowing in every sunrise and sunset, Millard Ridge overlooks the Badlands he loved and struggled to preserve. (1989, p. 35)

Chapter 9: The World War II Years – Ben and Stella Millard Face Years of Scarcity and Gas Rationing

Ben and Stella Millard's family had weathered the agricultural bust from 1919 through the mid-1930s, and the end of the 1930s found them well established in Cedar Pass Lodge. As I look back over outside reports and many letters between family and friends or business associates, I feel the most challenging period in their lives came five years after the death of Senator Norbeck (in 1936), with the start of the Second World War.

In 1946 Uncle Herb and park Custodian Howard Strickland had both returned from the service in the war. The Stricklands and the Millards worked well together and were good friends. Often at dinners I'd hear conversations about the problems with, for instance, cattle roaming freely and chewing on Uncle Herb's new trees. I found these conversations fascinating and I started to keep notes as well as copies of letters written to me by my Grandmother and Uncle Herb. I still refer to these notes and letters today. In addition to that, when I started researching this book, I began to contact friends of close South Dakota families from my generation whose parents were good friends of Grandfather or Grandmother. I owe them a great deal of gratitude for offering to part with copies of old letters received from Grandfather and Grandmother.[18]

Even though the Depression had seriously eaten into Cedar Pass Lodge's income, Grandfather felt he must continue to make improvements in conjunction with programs initiated by

---

18 Although our family did not seem to have a trove of personal family letters or documents from those days, I did receive a few letters and also was able to make some recordings of conversations with knowledgeable friends who had Badlands connections.

Roosevelt's New Deal, as described below. As the buildup to World War II continued at the end of the 1930s and into the 1940s, internal Millard family changes added more strain on Grandfather and Grandmother. All three of their close-knit offspring had moved on geographically: Glen had left first, twenty-five years earlier, to attend college, serve in the military, and enjoy a successful business career. Faye left home a couple years later and established herself in a "lettered" college as a counselor and administrator. Herbert was the last to venture out, attending college and working with Glen, but he was also the first to return and work in the family business.

All three Millard children went on to have successful business and social careers at removed locations in Chicago and Minnesota. Yet, one way or another, they did whatever they could to assist Grandmother and Grandfather during difficult years, and they kept in close contact with each other.

The eldest Millard son, Glen (my dad), graduated from Whittier High School in California. Glen had enrolled in Occidental College, and then received a PhB degree from the University of Chicago. He enlisted as a private in the US Infantry, attended US third officers school, was commissioned a second lieutenant in August 1918, and was stationed in Texas to train troops. After the end of the war, he returned to Chicago. At twenty-three years old, he became sales manager of the prominent investment banking firm A.G. Becker, where he worked for twelve years.[19] When the Depression hit, Glen was married with three children. He was also well

---

[19] Per Wikipedia, Becker's originated in the 1880s. Through the early part of the twentieth century, Becker became one of the leading commercial paper firms in the United States. Becker's commercial paper business had been founded on the dealing of "bankers acceptances," another form of short-term finance for corporate borrowers, which was popular in the Chicago markets. (A. G. Becker & Co., n.d.)

"schooled" about the Depression years. When A.G. Becker had to drastically cut back due to the Depression, Dad lost his job as sales manager and was "out on the street" in 1932.

As an entrepreneur, he was able to obtain—with the help of his two brothers-in-law—the necessary funds to take over a fledgling toothpaste manufacturer, Lactona, Inc., and he built the company up, making it one of the principal producers of US dental products. Lactona was very active and skilled in pioneering designs of toothbrushes for the professional dental society. He was inducted into the American Academy of Periodontology as their only lay member for the work he did in providing tools and information to assist in educating the public about good dental health. His whole life, my father maintained a love of music, drama, and the arts. These loves were ingrained in him from his summers at Ruskin Park.

Faye, who was born in Artesian, South Dakota, on Christmas Day of the first Christmas of the new century (1900), had moved to Chicago, attended the University of Chicago, and received a PhB in June of 1922.[20] While an undergraduate, Faye (later Faye Millard MacFarland) was very active in the university, serving as a member of the Ida Noyes Auxiliary, the Freshman Commission, the Ida Noyes Advisory Council, the Woman's Athletic Association (WAA), Dramatic Club, Federation Sponsor, Executive Council, Senior Vaudeville, and Nu Pi Sigma, among other organizations. The substantial and varied listing of papers written by Aunt Faye can be found through the University of Chicago Library.[21] Faye, along with the rest of the family, was a summer participant in live stage and, later, film performances at Ruskin Park.

---

[20] All three of the young Millards, Glen, Faye, and Herbert, graduated from the University of Chicago with PhB degrees (bachelor of philosophy degrees heavy on research efforts). Faye continued to be connected with the university, whereas her two brothers moved out of Chicago after graduating, though Glen returned after World War I and his military service.

[21] Some of her work is easily found online in the University of Chicago Library's "Guide to the Faye Millard Papers, 1927," which lists two boxes of papers covering an extensive range of subjects

(*Top to bottom*) Dad, Aunt Faye, Uncle Herb.

Herbert, born in 1902 in Artesian, South Dakota, spent his early childhood living winters in Whittier, California, and summers at Ruskin Park. Herbert's background demands the most detail out of the immediate family because he returned and worked at the Cedar Pass Loge and the Pinnacles gift shop. His specialty was in the substantial foraging and buying activities for the entire stock of gift shop items. His efforts, for example, resulted in Cedar Pass Lodge becoming one of the largest purchasers of high-quality, Two Grey Hills Trading Post (New Mexico) Navajo rugs and blankets. He also purchased large quantities of fine Navajo and Zuni jewelry. The relationship established with Victor Walker, the trading post representative, went on to be a family friendship that endured and helped Grandmother and Grandfather get through tough

(https://www.lib.uchicago.edu/e/scrc/findingaids/view.php?eadid=ICU.SPCL.MACFARLANDFM).

times. Vic and Herbert were close, longtime friends, and I was fortunate to often spend time with Victor too.

Herbert was twenty-six when he graduated from the University of Chicago in 1924. After working with his brother, Glen, in the early 1930s, he returned to South Dakota and was operating the Pinnacles with Grandmother when, in 1936, my sister and I made our first trip to visit the Badlands.

In 1942, although Herbert was forty years old, he volunteered for service in the US Navy Reserves. When he went to a local recruitment office, the recruitment officer, asked him, "What are we going to do with an Old F---t like you?" The situation was resolved after the man more carefully looked over Herb's resume and saw his experience, university grades, and so on. At that time, a high priority of the US Navy was to enlist people with proven managerial abilities. Herbert was a strong candidate because of his day-to-day managing of the substantial Cedar Pass Lodge staff. So, they signed Herb into the US Navy Reserves. He was commissioned a lieutenant for active duty, and gunnery officer was his area of specialty. His service included eight months on the battleship USS *New Mexico* (*BB-40*) where he supported the invasion of Okinawa and witnessed the Japanese surrender in Tokyo Bay.

After discharge, he returned to Cedar Pass Lodge where, as Grandfather was aging, Herbert began to manage more of the daily operations with the help of Grandmother and Herbert's wife , Dorothy Davis Millard[22]. Aunt Dorothy was definitely a stalwart favorite of the regular

---

[22] Dorothy La Rue Davis Millard, daughter of John Russell Davis and Nellie Strong Davis, was born in Lincoln, Nebraska on January 8, 1902, and married Herbert Millard on March 1, 1930. She received a BSc in education at the University of Nebraska in 1926 and became an Registered Nurse California in 1941.

staff in the lodge and cabin maintenance group. For years, she worked tirelessly as Grandmother's daughter-in-law with never a bad word passing between them.

1942, (left to right) Herb Millard, Grandmother Stella Neely, and Ben Millard.

When the Japanese bombed Pearl Harbor on December 7, 1941, Uncle Herb told my dad he was seriously considering volunteering for service in the US Navy. Our family in Minnesota had gotten to know and respect a WWI veteran, Emin Vitalis. Dad had concluded that Emin would be a great help for Grandmother and Grandfather at Cedar Pass to fill in for Uncle Herb. Emin Vitalis (Arthur Emin Vitalis), born in Franconia, Minnesota, in 1889, had moved to Cedar Pass from Franconia and became, in effect, a member of our family. He was a close friend of Grandfather's and a terrific addition to the crew. Emin was a World War I vet who had survived a poison gas attack, resulting in severe asthma. The high level of humidity in Minnesota was difficult for him, and my father, his longtime friend, suggested that he should consider moving to the Badlands. Dad told Emin he would be very pleased to make the introduction as Dad was

117

certain Emin would fit right in. That introduction was a really terrific break for all involved. Emin stayed at Cedar Pass Lodge the rest of his life until he passed away in 1957, just a year after Grandfather died. He was greatly missed by all, including me, as I had known Emin since about 1935 and often saw him at Cedar Pass Lodge.

Emin is buried in Franconia, Minnesota, where there is a wide-ranging group of Vitalis family relatives nearby. As kids back in the 1930s and early 1940s, we spent lots of time in the summers with Emin's nephews: Billy, Dale, and Jackie Vitalis in Franconia. Emin was, to all of us, one of the sweetest, friendliest people we knew, and he taught us all how to make whistles out of willow branches. He also amazed us with the fine carvings he made with his jackknife.

A lot of changes were going on in the surroundings of Cedar Pass Lodge and the NPS locations leading up to the US participation in World War II. These changes had very noticeable effects on the operations, owners, and employees of resorts in national monuments and national parks. Many projects were accomplished by agencies established by Franklin Roosevelt under executive orders to provide relief to farmers and ranchers as well as unemployed urban dwellers. Several of the projects had very favorable direct benefits for Grandfather who was managing and improving Cedar Pass Lodge full-time after 1936.

As outlined by the NPS in *The History of The Badlands National Monument*, some of the projects closely related to Cedar Pass Lodge are listed:

> Under the general direction of the NPS, various relief agencies such as the Emergency Relief Administration (ERA), the Resettlement Administration, the Works Progress Administration (WPA), and the Civilian Conservation Corps (CCC) worked on

development projects in the area. Only a few scattered reports are now available on the work of these agencies. About 150 persons were employed at the area in January 1937 on such projects as resurfacing, backsloping [banksloping], ditching, and grading roads. This included major reconstruction of the Sheep Mountain Canyon road, completed the same year.

One project of interest completed June 30, 1940 by ERA labor, under the Public Roads Administration, was the obliteration of two tunnels along the Pinnacles–Cedar Pass road. They were constructed during the first half of the 1930's when the road was built by the State of South Dakota; the road was completed in 1935. The tunnels proved to be impractical because of inadequate width and maintenance problems.

In July 1940 the ERA project in the area was discontinued. Among the types of work accomplished since July 1, 1936, when the project was initiated, were the construction of five project headquarters buildings, prospecting for water on the national monument, the development of a well near the site of the old Pinnacles Checking Station, and ten road jobs which included road construction, widening, graveling, building culverts, and banksloping. The construction of parking overlooks, and the obliteration of buildings and clearing of 16 farmstead tracts, also took place during that time. (Mattison & Grom, 1968, p. 43)

Then, the NPS made a major improvement in its operations that rubbed off on Cedar Pass Lodge. Chief Ranger Howard B. Stricklin of Wind Cave National Park became acting custodian of the newly designated area (I was fortunate enough to meet Howard and later his family). It's impossible to express how much that meant in terms of working and personal relationships between Cedar Pass Lodge and the NPS. I can recall Grandfather, Grandmother, and Uncle Herb, in particular, telling me time and again, what a terrific manager Ranger Stricklin was to work with. His arrival was as if a long lost friend or family relative had returned. He was very businesslike and listened to what the other side had to say in discussions to make fair decisions.

Since the national monument is located a relatively short distance from Wind Cave National Park, the older area coordinated the business of Badlands during its early years. On August 11, 1939, Chief Ranger Howard B. Stricklin of Wind Cave became acting custodian of the newly designated area and was later placed in charge of the local ERA and CCC projects. Although the ERA project was terminated in July 1940, the CCC work continued until June 1942.

When Stricklin arrived to take charge, there were no living quarters of any kind in the area. . . . Temporary offices were established in Wall pending a decision regarding the location of permanent headquarters.

Considerable thought was given to the selection of a headquarters site. For a time the Pinnacles area was considered. However, in late 1939 it was finally decided to locate the center of operations at Cedar Pass. This decision was due, in part, to the offer by Mr. Ben H. Millard, owner of Cedar Pass Lodge, to donate approximately 28 acres of strategically located land in the Cedar Pass area to the Service to be used as a headquarters area. The Department of the Interior accepted Millard's donation in May 1941.

One of the great handicaps of Cedar Pass as a headquarters area was the lack of water. To develop a satisfactory supply, the NPS found it necessary to go to the White River, three miles south. One of the major projects undertaken soon after selecting the headquarters site was to dig a trench and lay pipe to the river. . . . [Water] was pumped to a 100,000-gallon storage tank above the headquarters area. Work was begun on this reservoir in April 1940 and completed by the CCC in September 1941. At the same time the CCC also erected a checking station at Pinnacles which Stricklin and his family occupied from November 15, 1940, until about May 15, 1943.

At that time the only visitor-contact point in the Cedar Pass area was at Cedar Pass Lodge. During the summer season Mr. Millard lectured nightly to lodge guests on the geologic history of the Badlands, thereby initiating interpretive programs. He also showed movies of the Badlands and other scenic areas. A temporary park ranger, who checked travel in the Cedar Pass area during the day, took part in the evening programs. (Mattison & Grom, 1968, pp. 42-45)

Another major problem encountered early on for both the NPS and the Cedar Pass Lodge was the wandering cattle, inside and outside boundaries. It had been a long-standing practice of some ranchers to let their cattle browse on the short but very nutritious buffalo grass, which grows very well in many parts of the Badlands.

The plentiful buffalo grass in the Badlands was both a plus and a minus for the NPS and our family. These grasses supported buffalo, deer, antelope, bighorn sheep, and many other native animals. The problem was that cattle also coveted it.

The lodge, with the NPS office and visitor complex, was trying to grow some shade trees, of which there were very few any distance from water. Every evening when the baking sun started to cool, it was necessary to water young trees until they could sink roots deep. The cattle loved the nice, green, moist leaves. Stricklin wrote of his concern:

> The problem of stock grazing in the national monument grew increasingly worse during the 1940s. The acting custodian complained early in 1940:
>
> > Until the boundary is fenced and we are in a better position to know what is private and what is monument land, there appears to be very little that can be done to prevent this.
>
> In December 1941, he wrote in a similar vein:
>
> > During past winters it has been the practice of local stockmen to allow herds of horses and cattle to drift into the monument area to graze unrestrictedly over public as well as private lands and along the monument highways. There is such a large amount of private and county-owned land within the monument boundaries (31,000 acres out of a total of 150,000) that it is difficult to restrain stock from grazing on National Park Service land as well as on the land that is owned or leased by private individuals. (Mattison & Grom, 1968, p. 45)

By the 1940s, a major NPS policy decision from 1929 had transformed the Badlands into a world-class national monument. The decision, called "Master Planning", was made at the top of NPS and challenged everyone involved in NPS projects to conserve the natural landscape they were working in. The mandate had two major effects: (1) It solidified the question of whether or not Cedar Pass Lodge and the adjacent land should be continued as the headquarters area of the national monument and later of the national park. (2) Its defining principles later became the reason to approve Senator Norbeck and Ben's common vison and foresight on road and site layouts, use of local materials, grouping of buildings, and, most of all, fitting the structures into the landscape and allowing or permitting tourists and visitors the best view possible.

The *Milner Report* describes exactly what Master Planning means:

> The New Deal Era (1929–1941): Master Planning within the NPS became a mandatory process in 1929 under the leadership of landscape architect Thomas Vint. Principles established in 1916 that centered on landscape preservation and conservation determined policies that guided all future planning. Key park service personnel including the NPS Director, Stephen Mather, landscape architect, Thomas Vint, and others, determined that in order to conform to principles of preservation and conservation of the natural landscape, construction was to disturb the ground as little as possible and improvements were to be of native materials, and rustic in character. This concept was particularly prevalent in national parks in the west where landscape architects struggled to plan necessary visitor facilities in landscapes that encompassed vast areas of natural scenery. (Bahr, Vermeer, & Haecker Architects, Ltd., in association with John Milner Associates, Inc., and Renewable Technologies, Inc., 2006, p. 240)

The application of Master Planning is seen in the consideration given to whether the monument headquarters' current location was the best choice among the many. It was favored because of the gorgeous view and panorama at the Pinnacles, as well as the fact that the land to build had been donated. Arguments against it were lack of space to expand, proximity to the vistas, lack of available water, and the need for staff and employees to live outside the monument boundary in Wall or elsewhere.

At that point in 1940 and 1941, tourist traffic had held up well. In fact, even though of the approximately seventy total miles within the monument, only about thirty miles were gravel, and the other forty odd were dirt, "thousands of travelers turned off the through highways to view the scenic Badlands" (Mattison & Grom, 1968, p.46).

Manager Stricklin reported in September 1941:

More than a quarter of a million visitors had passed through Badlands National Monument by the close of the travel season on September 30, representing an increase of approximately 30 percent over the previous year, for the period during which an actual count was made. (Mattison & Grom, 1968, p. 46)

In the first two years of the war, the alphabet agencies ended their major construction projects in the park.

The entrance of the United States into World War II in December 1941 had a great impact on the area and its operations. Since many of the CCC enrollees would be absorbed into the armed forces, the project work soon came to an end. The acting custodian reported in the spring of 1942, "On March 25, after two years and five months of productive work in Badlands National Monument, CCC Camp Badlands, NP-3 [located at Cedar Pass], was abandoned." Work was continued on several projects undertaken at Camp Badlands by a CCC side camp with the view toward completing the projects or leaving them "in such condition that the facilities involved may be used, and the materials, all of which have been on hand for some time, may be protected against deterioration and loss." However, the side camp was also closed in the following June, leaving practically all of the construction projects in various states of completion. In December 1942 most of the CCC buildings at Cedar Pass were dismantled and removed by the armed services. (Mattison & Grom, 1968, p. 46)

The numbers of visitors entering the park changed with the onset of World War II as well:

Another result of the nation's entrance into the war was a sharp drop in visitors to the Badlands. Stricklin wrote in June 1942 that "Most of these visitors appeared to be genuine vacationists . . . [who] had a vacation coming, and were trying to get it in before gas rationing became nation-wide." He estimated that travel in March 1943 was 87 percent under that for March 1942, and that "All foreign [out-of-state] visitor cars stopping for information were headed for defense jobs, or were military personnel, changing their headquarters from one part of the country to another." (Mattison & Grom, 1968, p. 46)

Work in the Cedar Pass Lodge and NPS operations also settled into a slower routine.

Efforts at the national monument during the war were devoted largely to preventive maintenance. Changing his headquarters from Pinnacles to Cedar Pass in June 1943,

Stricklin was able to give closer attention to the headquarters area. Such routine tasks as filling washouts, cleaning ditches, reclaiming gravel, cutting roadside weeds, repairing guard rails, cleaning up debris, and temporary patching of roads occupied most of the staff's time. Other tasks, such as repairing water lines, painting signs, keeping the buildings in repair, and servicing and repairing the area equipment also required much attention. The cottage that the custodian and his family rented from Millard at Cedar Pass was destroyed by fire on November 27, 1943. (Mattison & Grom, 1968, p. 46)

Appendix A in the *History of the Badlands National Monument* book shows the total visitors for each year. The numbers from 1941 to 1945 are sobering.

1941	252,878
1942	87,231
1943	10,149
1944	10,349
1945	31,377
1946	230,403 (Mattison & Grom, 1968, p. 65)

The question for Cedar Pass Lodge would have been how many of those visitors actually stopped for an overnight visit or stopped at all even for a cup of coffee or a pair of baby Minnetonka Moccasins for a new grandchild present. By 1947, the visitation numbers shot back up to prewar levels.

Through some personal family letters shown a bit later in this chapter, it's clear that even with all the stresses of the times, Grandfather demonstrated his continued vision in the improvement and construction of buildings that then became a model for future developments within the overall National Park System.

> Millard remodeled several cabins in 1941, added plumbing, and constructed one new cabin. When he constructed a sewer line from Cedar Pass Lodge, intending to connect it with the NPS sewer system, CCC crews constructed a pipeline ditch from the reservoir at Cedar Pass to the highway, crossing at the junction of the highway and the headquarters area service road. In May 1941, Millard donated 160 acres that enabled the NPS to construct a custodian's residence at Cedar Pass. Although the land was located close to the formations, it became the beginning of the headquarters' residential area. At the same time, Millard continued to actively develop the area, laying cement asbestos pipes to the reservoir and constructing septic and dosing tanks that would eventually constitute the sewer system at Cedar Pass headquarters. (Bahr, Vermeer, & Haecker Architects, Ltd., in association with John Milner Associates, Inc., and Renewable Technologies, Inc., 2006, p. 244)

The following are selected personal letters that give a picture of the conditions of the time, including weather, roads, lack of supplies, and difficulties locating needed supplies. (My comments and additional observations appear in *italics*.)

Stoicism is a trait found in folks that have to learn to accommodate themselves to the conditions. However, one of my absolutely favorite mannerisms of my Grandmother Neno was her sarcastic and funny sense of humor. For example, if we were in the car, driving on slippery dirt roads, quite far removed from any houses or help, she might observe, "It would be a joke on us if we went off the road." Her sense of humor has stayed with me for eighty years and has helped me get through some very dicey situations.

Letter #1 – Grandmother to My Father (Glen): Written from the Pinnacles, April 29, 1942

Even though the darkness of the night will not let me sleep, I keep thinking of you and though I wonder I solve nothing. I sincerely hope everything is well and wish you as it can be in these times. Once it was important to keep in contact with you but wider and wider grows the chasm. Perhaps sometime I shall not be able to cross it. There are many things that I am grateful for. As to business, why worry. Surely it is beyond that now. I simply must trust, that's all. At present Cedar Pass looks impossible. Boy [*Grandmother's nickname for Ben*] has been putting in that sewer and the whole premises are dug up. The government did not get theirs completed and it's been raining. The ditches are full and, so much work. Bye Painter took a job at Rapid City for the summer [*Bye Painter was a principle jack-of-all-trades for Grandfather, Grandmother, and Cedar Pass. Bye worked on everything and was exceedingly reliable.*], and now I know Boy is overworking Emin Vitalis. Boy does not work so terribly hard but he gets very nervous. . . . Herbert and I have been down to Cedar Pass for weeks helping to get things organized and it's very hard work.[23] Herbert has been quite miserable. He had to go to Rapid City to the doctor. He's a bit better now.

[*They are getting ready to open for the season up there, but they go down to Cedar Pass. In those days, when the road was open after 1936, the trip was still on a gravel road,*

---

[23] Neno and Herbert were running the Pinnacles shop and living in the cabin, which was part of the Pinnacles complex. They were helping to get Cedar Pass Lodge set for opening the first part of May as the letter was written April 29th.

and it took a while to get down there. It wasn't something you could do in fifteen minutes; it was an hour or close to it. It seemed like it was hours when we were kids driving from the Pinnacles store to Cedar Pass Lodge.]

Rain, rain, it rained terrifically at Cedar Pass this evening. A little after six even threw a few hailstones. When it eased up we came home as we had Michael Stricklin (Howard Stricklin's son) [*Howard was the park superintendent, and he and his family were then living in Wall.*] with us and we thought that his parents would be frantic, but the storm had not come within ten miles of the Pinnacles. We left Boy [*at Cedar Pass Lodge*] working at the ditches in the pouring rain. But I hear it raining now (11 pm) this letter sounds like I feel-incoherent for short as of straight thinking. Time out for now for a word from you and my love to you. Signed Stella.[24]

[Continued on a P.S. page] May first. It began raining Wednesday evening and has not stopped for a minute, not yet. Friday noon the roads are so slippery we cannot get to town. I am anxious to learn what the water may have done to Boy's ditches – Evening. Herbert went to Cedar Pass with Howard. He found Boy and Emin okay and not so much damage by the rain this time. The White River down by Interior is the highest in 30 years. [*There were yet no telephones at either the Pinnacles or at Cedar Pass Lodge. The only way they could communicate would have been for Herbert to go to Wall and call Joe or Mable Haight in Interior—when their hardware store was open—and ask Joe to either go out to Cedar Pass Lodge or find someone who would. They would do it in reverse if Grandfather needed to get in touch with Herbert or Neno.*]

---

[24] "Stella" is the name Grandma used among close friends and family. To me, she was Neno.

Letter #2 – Uncle Herb to Chuck Orelup:[25] Written from the Pinnacles, August 16, 1942

Dear Chuck,

I have an option on a case of Super X Shells. I was wondering if you wanted these. I believe that I will have plenty for my own use because my shooting will be pretty well limited. At best I won't get to go more than once. If you want any or all these shells, let me know and I will buy them. Case price is around $27. I would like to have Clarence Choos get a few boxes too. Come down sometime and we will limber up our shooting eyes.

[*When there was time, Grandfather used to go with me to go hunting sharp-tailed grouse or prairie chickens at Louie Herscher's place, the rancher that we all liked so well (more about him later). Pheasants or grouse were a real treat for Grandmother.*]

Letter #3 – Grandmother to Chuck Orelup: Written from Cedar Pass Lodge, March 2, 1943

[*This is a note about the pheasants Chuck Orelup brought them that they appreciated so much.*]

When I returned from the basketball tournament at the hall on Saturday I found the grand pheasants that you sent us. How they do make me long for that. Herbert could help us cook a grand dinner. [*Herbert by now had volunteered and was in the US Navy as a gunnery officer.*] We thank you so much. We started to Rapid City Thursday and got

---

[25] Charles "Chuck" or "Charlie" Orelup owned and managed Rise Studio in Rapid City and was technically skilled as a photographer, producing most all of the postcards that Cedar Pass Lodge sold. He was definitely a *very* close friend of the entire family. He was also an avid hunter, so he and Uncle Herb took me antelope hunting and occasionally pheasant and sharp-tailed grouse hunting in the Badlands. The family relied on Chuck for all sorts of errands in Rapid City because trips there, although reasonably frequent, were a day's event. Chuck's Cadillac was usually dust covered from trips out to shoot gophers or prairie dogs on ranches. The car was often open and, in back, two or three rifles with scopes on them were in plain view, prepared for his next outing. Grandfather and Grandmother were also Cadillac owners. All three of them said Cadillacs were the most reliable for their long trips.

about three and a half or four miles from the Pinnacle and the clutch went out. Harry Johnson [*mechanic*] was supposed to try to find about it today. You may believe me I am weary being shut in down here. There is no word from Herbert yet but I haven't heard of any calamities his way so maybe Davy Jones is waiting for him. Boy walked towards Howard's, [*Stricklin's place in Wall*] and Howard met him coming this way so Howard pulled us to Wall and the car is there. I think someone could get the repairs if they put themselves to the bother. Boy isn't much of a pusher along that line. I think the clutch will have to be relined. How I wish we had got to Rapid City. We could have come home on the train. There is quite a fire hazard to have it in that building at the hall. I feel so bad about it all.

Letter #4 – Grandmother to Chuck Orelup: Written from Cedar Pass Lodge, March 19 (the envelope is dated March 20, 1943)

Dear Charles,

Your very much appreciated letter came today and you know it made me weep. I have been so disturbed over the car and for some reason it seemed too much effort for Boy to keep after it. I have a few times wondered secretly if he intended to get it fixed, but to stay walled in here has almost disturbed my point of view. I don't ever come to life.

[*At this point in 1943, Grandfather is now close to seventy and can't do as much as he used to.*]

Letter #5 – Grandmother to Chuck Orelup: Written from Cedar Pass Lodge, June 15, 1943[26]

---

[26] Chuck Orelup's son, Robert, thoughtfully gave these letters to me when I visited him in Rapid City in the summer

[Grandmother was writing Chuck about a very necessary item in a lodge with several cabins—an iron for ironing pillowcases and clothing. It was a vexing process to get repairs, and Chuck always helped them in an upbeat way, never complaining except in jest.]

Whatever is wrong with the iron I do not know. It started off well, heated fully, and then I pushed the switch as usual from linen to cotton and no more heat. That's the same thing it did before. I'm wondering if there's something wrong in the switch that it slips, the wire cord in the iron or what. If you know anyone that I could send it to, please suggest.

[So they write back and forth about just the iron so that she can get the iron repaired and allow her or one of the staff to iron some of the sheets and pillowcases for the cabins. Grandmother is younger than Grandfather but not by much. She's getting up there too at this point and is, I believe, 60 years old in 1943.]

Letter #5a – Grandmother to Chuck Orelup: Written from Cedar Pass Lodge, June 15, 1943

[This letter gives you an idea of how they made do with what they had.]

Dear Charles,

Thanks a million for the repair work on the iron. I've been hoping for some packs. Send 50 of the Badlands 1620, and 25 of the Black Hills 1650. Those are card numbers. [How does this film business run? She's trying to get film in this.] If your quota gets larger

---

of 2015 in an effort to find out who had bought Rise Studio when Chuck died. I wasn't able to find out after several leads failed. However, Robert told me to contact Joe Tlustos, formerly of SD Public Radio, and Ken Stewart, Director of Digital Archives, SD History Department (both of whom were very helpful and made introductions for me). That contact led me back to Ruskin Park and Ben and Helen Zoss, present owners of the former Ruskin Park land.

because some customers might be out of business, would others get more? We will be short on 120, 620 and 127, long on 122. Okay on 116 and maybe okay on 616. [*Those are the film numbers for the Brownie Cameras we carried and were what the vast percentage of tourists brought with them, particularly the kids.*] The Pinnacles caught hail again on Sunday and it will have to have a new roof and some windows. I brought my card display rack here to see what I can do for the picture business. You know we had a $150 day on Sunday; ten cents today. Thank Charles for your time and labor. Enclosed at least for the postage.

Letter #6 – Grandfather to Chuck Orelup: Written from Cedar Pass Lodge, July 12, 1943

Dear Charlie,

Please send us 50 Badlands packets, 25 cents size, and 50 Badlands packets, 50 cents size. I think those are little packets of cards smaller than the postcards. If you like, you may send us what 8mm colored movie film you think you would like to sell. I got three the other day when I was there and I am now sold out. Whatever you send will be greatly appreciated. Sometime when you are out on the street see if you can get me two #80539 motor belts for Stewart. The model number belts now on the refrigerator, #MW454 belts. I think the Modern Equipment Company handles the Stewart Warner refrigerator; at least they did at the time. They are located on St. John Street, west from the hill.

Letter #7 – Grandmother to Chuck Orelup: Written from Cedar Pass Lodge, January 7, 1943

Dear Charles,

[They must have had an accident in the car.]

Thanks a lot for your letter. Our car has only body damages. I think it seems to run smoothly and no extra noises. We had planned to come to Rapid today but it looked stormy and snowed some. Howard said this PM that the roads were slippery too. We have not recovered from the rollover that the embankment caused. I'm glad we did not go over it. Another fellow got a terrible shakeup the same night. It was terribly slippery.

Letter #8 – Grandmother to Chuck Orelup: Written from Cedar Pass Lodge, April 9, 1943

Dear Charles,

Your card came today. It was grand of you to be smart enough to order a battery from Montgomery Ward. I am only sorry to put you to the bother but I am glad your head still works.

He had planned to go to R.C. today but this slippery Badland road is slippery. He will likely get down next week so just hold the battery until we come.

Boy is working on his garden and has onions, radishes and peas peeping thru. They may get their peppers nipped.

The extent and depth of the changes felt by Grandfather and Grandmother during the period in the first couple years of 1940s is difficult to imagine now. Cedar Pass Lodge and the NPS headquarters had benefited by all the infrastructure projects completed by the CCC and WPA. At the same time, Grandfather tied his private development projects with the government activity, such as connecting sewer and electrical lines with new lines laid by the CCC. It was a

134

whirlwind time of work that left the two complexes ready, able, and willing to greet increased tourist visits. However, the entrance of the United States into World War II dashed those high hopes.

Grandfather continued to donate land parcels throughout the period for the NPS headquarters area and for the new Badlands Loop Road to permit improved Badlands scenery viewing for travelers and tourists.

At the same time, our government was hard at work trying to prepare the US public for the likely (and weekly increase in probability) entrance of our military into the conflict. The sentiment was causing national shifts in employment as "Rosie the Riveter" ads showed huge increases of women in the workforce beginning well before the Japanese attack on Pearl Harbor.

> Rosie the Riveter is a cultural icon of World War II, representing the woman who worked in factories and shipyards during World War II, many of whom produced munitions and war supplies. These women sometimes took entirely new jobs replacing the male workers who joined the military. Rosie the Riveter is used as a symbol of American Feminism and women's economic advantage. (Rosie the Riveter, n.d.)

The next World War II whammy that hit was rationing, which was no small consideration for a tourist resort providing full menus along with overnight accommodations. The following list of rationed items provides a glimpse into how obtaining supplies in a remote, rural area often became very complicated and was accompanied by long delays or necessary substitutions.

While some food items were scarce, others did not require rationing, and Americans adjusted accordingly. "Red Stamp" rationing covered all meats, butter, fat, and oils, and with some exceptions, cheese. Each person was allowed a certain amount of points weekly with expiration dates to consider. "Blue Stamp" rationing covered canned, bottled, frozen fruits and vegetables, plus juices and dry beans, and such processed foods as soups, baby food and ketchup. (Online Highways LLC, 2019)

One last personal view to note is that I recall the steps my father and mother took to help the war effort, as nearly everyone pitched in. My father insisted we even save tinfoil chewing gum wrappers (if we could buy gum). We had to flatten down the wrappers and save them. Mother went through pots and pans to see which metal ones were being called for and then donated them. Dad ended up as a member of the War Production Board after his company, Lactona, figured out a way to select, clean, and use domestic pig bristles for making paintbrushes up to US Navy specifications.

The sum total of all these changes added a lot of challenges to an already tough business environment, considering the 600 percent drop in traffic the park saw after 1941.

Chapter 10: Life at the Lodge, Inside and Outside, Heralded Out Front by Dewey and Alice Beard's Tepee

In the memories of my youth, the days began cool and early in the Badlands. The sky was clear, and the air was dry. The first, early-bird tourists are rushing to get to the Black Hills and beyond. They are up and on their way—awake even before the meadowlarks, which were perched, rocking back and forth, on the reasonably loose wire fence. The fence had been designed to keep the wandering cattle from eating the green leaves on the small trees and flowers Uncle Herb had watered the evening before, but the sumptuous delicacies were too tempting. Large cows stretched the wire almost to the breaking point but couldn't quite manage to taste the fruits of their labors. Yet all was not lost as their calves, close behind them, could easily get at the greens. I see clearly, Uncle Herb, on his way back from starting the old diesel generator, striding toward his fence with rake in hand to chase away unlucky calves that crawled under his patented fence. Like the early birds, he was starting his day at the break of dawn.

My wife Patty and I were frequently fortunate to be able to visit Grandfather, Grandmother, and Uncle Herb at the same time that Aunt Faye was there visiting. Often while I was working for Western Airlines in Huron, South Dakota, or in Denver, Colorado, my wife and I would visit Cedar Pass during their off-seasons. We both are indebted to Aunt Faye for life for translating the meadowlarks song as "Nothing to Do Today." One does not even have to listen closely, as many visitors to Cedar Pass can attest, because the meadowlarks put all their energy, lung power, heart, and soul into announcing their plans for the day to all nearby. It takes a strong voice to advise people what to do today when you are only a medium-sized songbird and you want to make sure everyone hears your plans. It's easy to observe the energy they put into it, swinging back and forth, perched on Uncle Herb's wire cattle fence as they belt out "Nothing to Do Today."

One of my most significant memories of Cedar Pass is the early morning image and sound of the meadowlarks as Patty, Aunt Faye, and I stood outside. We tracked the sun as it crept over Millard Ridge while quietly sipping fresh cups of coffee brewed for us by Joe, the chef. The three of us and the meadowlarks were "Comp visitors," without specific jobs so we felt a companionship or solidarity with the meadowlark in thinking of what to do.

For many years, travel to Cedar Pass Lodge wasn't the only way to hear the meadowlarks greet the day, as we had lots of them in rural areas of Minnesota. But they have deserted us, I guess. So now, even though our family no longer tends to the cows, as Uncle Herb and Park Superintendent Stricklin used to, I am compelled, by my soul, to go once a year and listen to the meadowlarks. That may be the real reason I have spent five years researching and writing this book.

Later in this chapter, I've listed all sorts of other reasons to return, such as prowling the Buffalo National Grasslands to see if I'm lucky enough to find even a tiny Fairburn agate. Hundreds, if not thousands, of other rock hounds and tourists continue to search for agates, petrified wood, other minerals, and fossils. For a complete Badlands experience, my advice is to stay overnight and get up just as the cool of the night is dissipating. Make a nice cup of coffee or some green tea with jasmine, go outside, and listen carefully. The meadowlarks will tell you how they plan to spend their day, singing before the grasshoppers even start moving around. While finishing your drink, you can conjure up your own day's plan. Fill your itinerary with enjoying the spectacular scenery, soaking up the great weather, or observing the incredible variety of wildlife that declare the Badlands a paradise.

By 7:00 a.m. or so, hungry visitors are looking frantically for a cup of coffee or Native American tea. I invite you to imagine that you are speeding into the Badlands. An excited child asks, "When are we ever going to stop? You promised that we could stop somewhere in the Badlands and have pancakes and maple syrup and chocolate milk. Well, look down below. There are those cabins and a lodge that looks like a dining room, and there is an Indian chief and his wife with their tepee. Can't we stop there?" Well, it goes something like that, between 50 to 500 times a day in the summer when close to a million visitors a year pass through the Badlands National Park.

The park guide shows that the Badlands National Park Visitors Center is open in the summer from 7:00 a.m. to 7:00 p.m. The park rangers at the front desk are great and like kids, which is good news for traveling families. Just to the left as visitors come in the front door, the bookstore has all kinds of fascinating books, maps, postcards, and more. If Katie Johnston, the executive director of the Badlands Natural History Association, is there, travelers are in luck because she knows more about the Badlands than I could ever guess. Her grandmother was an old friend of our family, and Katie has expended much effort working on projects to help people understand things like what these strange formations are, how they got this way, and whether anything will grow on them.

Travelers could also continue down the road a couple hundred yards and go inside Cedar Pass Lodge for the pancakes with maple syrup or the famous Sioux Indian taco of spiced buffalo meat on fry bread (reviewed by one savvy traveler as the best meal on their entire seven-week trip).

A Grandson's View from Inside the Lodge

When I was sixteen (1946), I was given the opportunity to fly out[27] to South Dakota to spend a week or two alone with Grandmother, Grandfather, Uncle Herb, Aunt Dorothy, and Emin Vitalis—the extended family. Herbert was back from his service in the US Navy and was handling more and more management duties in the lodge, particularly the store. However, the size and scope of Cedar Pass Lodge required all of them to care for customers when it was busy.

There were a number of key employees helping out at Cedar Pass. Rilla and Albert Thompson came in every day to help in the store. They, too, were like members of the family. Tom and Martha Boothroyd, from St. George, Utah, were also part of the crew. Tuesy Johnson[28] managed the overnight cabins' daily maintenance and readied them for new guests each night. Tuesy's son, Lester Johnson, who was about my age, worked like his mother, Tuesy, who was filled with amazing energy! Lester was a nice guy, and we had a chance now and then to jabber. But while the cabins were being cleaned, there was no letup with this amazing crew. Neno and Aunt Dorothy felt fortunate to have two Native American women working for them in the lodge

---

[27] For my first airline flights, Mother and Dad drove me down to Rochester, Minnesota, or somewhere south, and I flew out in a Lockheed plane similar to the plane Amelia Earhart flew. Knowing that certainly didn't make me more relaxed on the flight.

[28] Tuesy Johnson's sister-in-law, Fern, was postmistress of Interior, South Dakota, for many years, and their daughter Faith worked at the Lodge.

and on the cabin crew. Theresa Fire Thunder and Celane[29] (Dewey Beard's granddaughter) were two of Aunt Dorothy and Grandmother's favorite longtime employees.

(Left to right) Mabel Haight, Rilla Thompson,
Albert Thompson, Joe Haight.

With the staff of dedicated, hardworking, and good-natured crew inside and outside the lodge, it was not surprising that the place ran so well and continued to look so good, although some of the cabins and buildings had been there for quite a few years. (The new cabins, which I saw in 2017, were impressive.) I feel a sense of gratitude to all the crew with whom I made good memories back in the 1940s and 1950s. Aunt Dorothy acted as a co-manager in the store and was always cheerful and hardworking.

---

[29] Celane was married to a Native American man whose last name was "Not Help Him," as reported by Gordon Hanson, a *Rapid City Journal* staff writer, in an article entitled "Beard artifacts questioned" published on December 26, 1991. The article refers to an auction of Dewey Beard's clothing and relics.

A final mention of the longest time family employee is due here. One of Neno's closest staff, Marie Bradley, was a nursing assistant to Neno at the birth of Uncle Herb in 1902. When I spent extended periods of time at Cedar Pass Lodge 40 to 50 years later, Marie was still working with the cabin staff and helping Neno seven days a week. Marie was partially handicapped with a bad leg and a very noticeable limp. But that, in no way, indicated that she couldn't do the job of a full-time employee. Obviously, she was a great help to the family as she was implicity trusted and relied upon after all those years.

Although cars would stream by each day in the summer shortly after first light with early-bird travelers, our long days officially began at 7:00 a.m. starting mid-May and continuing into the last day of August. However, though I don't remember the actual closing time back in the 1940s, the current schedule states the dining room stays open until 9:00 p.m. through the month of August. I recall vividly that it was well past dark when we began to do the last chores of the day. The front door was locked each night after the last guests in the tourist shop and dining room had left. Then, we had to balance or close out the day for the cash receipts. Grandfather, Emin, Uncle Herb, Aunt Dorothy, and I would separate the coins and each take some to count. Next, Uncle Herb, Aunt Dorothy, or Emin would count the bills. Grandmother would be straightening out the small office and gift-wrapping area right next to or alongside where we did the counting. Grandfather would check the total against the receipts. After that, as if the climax of a dinner party, we would all have ice cream or a snack while Grandfather and Emin had grapefruit with salt on it.

Depending on whether there were any calamities that had to be taken care of right away or the plans that needed to be written for the first thing the next morning, the workday ended around 10 p.m.

The start of the day was early for Uncle Herb, around 5 a.m., a couple hours before the store opened. Grandmother would also be up early to dust the jewelry cases inside and out. There was always a small amount of dust that would find its way in due to all the traffic going in and out of the front lodge door, plus the air conditioning was continuously blowing all day. During the day Aunt Dorothy, Neno, and Rilla and Albert Thompson were the salespeople, although Uncle Herb was the most familiar with the jewelry and the Navajo rugs as he had done the buying with Victor Walker.

Making sure that the inventory in the store was complete was a steady job. The start of each day was an inventory event. Every item had a tag on it, which told the retail price on front. On the back of each tag was a code recording the price we had paid for it.

Doing this seven days a week, fifteen hours a day, was exhausting, especially because the whole time is spent standing, let alone the extra hours before and after the regular opening and closing time. Now and then, some customers with cabin reservations misjudged the driving time and arrived late. Uncle Herb would open up and get them to their cabin. He had a strong sense of empathy for traveling families, and he knew finding a vacancy during peak season might require a long drive late at night. I heard an example of this happening from grandmother. As the story goes, Uncle Herb met a family late, which turned out to be a large family, and the father didn't have enough money to afford lodging. Uncle Herb not only gave him the room on credit, but also gave the man some money. The family had not eaten dinner, so the father used a little gas stove and he cooked on the floor of the cabin. As murphy's law would have it, things went wrong, and he burned a hole in the cabin floor. The man was terribly embarrassed, but he had to report to Herbert the next morning. He promised to pay for the damage and Uncle Herb loaned him even more money. The man paid back every cent over a period of time.

Theoretically, I was the "cabin boy" whenever I was there. Uncle Herb would ask me to show the guests to their cabins and make sure everything was okay. This meant walking or running down to the cabins ahead of the visitors in their cars to show them which cabin was theirs and where to park. Uncle Herb had plenty to do, and I'm sure he must have been exasperated with me when I wasn't nearby in the late afternoon or early evening. He was always direct but gracious in his explanation to me that he depended on my being available to show visitors their cabins for the evening instead of spending that time talking to girls.

It was a dream job. In addition to my work as cabin boy, I worked inside the store. They educated me in the Navajo and Zuni jewelry. Neno, especially, was always ready to joke about something or go along with an idea to have fun while working. For example, one of the constant top sellers was the inexpensive "Indian" tom-tom drum. The tom-toms came in three or four sizes and were made by Bloom Brothers Co. of Minneapolis to look like real Indian drums. The tom-toms consisted of an interior coffee can with inner tube–like rubber stretched over the top and bottom. The coffee can sides were covered with some kind of tough paper or fabric with an appropriate design. Small holes were punched in the rubber tops and bottoms and laced tightly to hold the rubber and the side coverings on. Finally, colored Indian designs or figures were painted on the center tops and bottom rubber. Attached to the tom-tom, a stick with a little rawhide pouch on the end was made to simulate a drumstick.

Bloom Brothers had developed a huge business and were pioneers in the wholesale trade to tourist stores across the United States. The tom-toms were a hot souvenir item for kids. A good tourist shop in any area frequented by families had to provide some lower priced items, but that didn't rule out stores' ability to also sell fine jewelry, woven goods, and authentic artisan goods.

So, Neno and I, when we hit quiet periods in the store, would make a triangular tower of the tom-toms. Then, she and I would wager candy or ice cream or something with each other on various tests. For example, we'd guess how long it would take before someone would want one of the bottom drums, necessitating taking apart our pyramid. Or, we'd each pick out a tom-tom and wager on which color would sell first. It was a sociology experiment, not at all at the expense of the buyers. We knew it was a really popular item, and the kids loved them. The bad part, I thought, must have been when the families left the lodge and climbed into their cars without air conditioning. The children were now holding pop bottles, melting ice cream cones, and little drums to bang on. All these years later, I still speculate on the mayhem, having taken innumerable automobile trips with our four young kids and seen it all several times.

Grandma (Neno) holding great grandson Ben Millard
with dog Radee helping.

In a lot of ways, Grandmother held the place together. If nothing else, she was a key manager of the lodge. Her organizational abilities facilitated repairs and the completion of urgent projects.

On the first floor of the lodge in the southeastern corner of the building, there was an old pantry and former kitchen, which was Grandmother's private kitchen domain and storage area. As far as I could tell, everyone left that area to her control. She knew which drawers, shelves, and cabinets held specific tools or supplies. When Uncle Herb, (and sometimes Grandfather), would be called to solve some minor, urgent—but critical—repair and needed some specialize tool, tape, or type of fastener, he would ask Neno if she knew where one was. It was great fun to watch as she gave Herbert her quizzical stare as if trying to recollect and then would reply, "Well I think I might be able to find one. Tell me where you'll be for the next few minutes and I will let you know." The chances are in the 90 to 100 percent range that she knew the exact location of whatever Uncle Herb was after because a month or so earlier, he had been required to fix a similar situation. Upon completion of that repair, he had been called away for some other problem and left the tool behind. The whole purpose of her apparent uncertainty and request for a few minutes to search was a well-practiced charade on her part to keep the supplicant from learning where she kept such treasures, so the next time someone needed that item, Grandmother would be able to solve his problem. In this sense, her concealed tools and so on were comparable to what a mission commander would consider as essential or never-to-be-left-behind necessities when traveling, for example, to Antarctica or outer space. In the 1940s and beginning of the 1950s, when I often spent time at Cedar Pass, I realized how difficult and time-consuming it must have been for Neno to replace her hidden treasures when necessary, given the inconvenience of no telephones, no electricity, and hundreds of tourists coming in daily.

It turned out that she had even squirreled away some powdered malted mix drink. One afternoon, she led me to the kitchen and asked if I didn't think it was a good idea for the two of us to make a chocolate malted milk. Out of her secret stash, she produced an old handheld electric blender. That soon became an occasional treat for the two of us—now and then we invited Grandfather, Uncle Herb, Aunt Dorothy, and Emin to join us.

Herbert and Dorothy Millard at Cedar Pass Lodge holding
Ben Herbert Millard, great-grandson of Ben Millard.
Summer of 1959. The dog's name is April.

I would be remiss were I to leave the impression that Grandmother was occupied only with

light work inside in what she and I called her "pack rat den" (kitchen).[30] Many times, I saw her

out back in the morning bending over one of the old metal washtubs using a big stick shaped

like a paddle to clean and sanitize bed linens or busy making soap from fat she had saved and

mixed with lye. She'd be outside, just as the morning cool was dissipating, but before the

midday sun started baking the driveway. Her timing was perfect because when the sun had

---

[30] "Pack rats [the rodent kinds] are nest builders. They use plant material such as twigs, sticks, and other available debris. They are particularly fond of shiny objects. A peculiar characteristic is that if they find something they want, they will drop what they are currently carrying—for example, a piece of cactus—and 'trade' it for the new item. They can also be quite vocal and boisterous. Getting into everything from attics to car engines, stealing their 'treasures', damaging electrical wiring, and creating general noisy havoc can easily cause them to become a nuisance." The article refers to their nests as "dens" (Pack rat, n.d.).

begun to warm the day, a breeze would start up, allowing her to hang up the clean wash to dry and get the fresh air scent. She also knew to stretch the sheets and pillowcases and tightly fasten them to the line, so the wind would shake out most of the wrinkles.

Grandfather's public schedule began every morning when guests came to the dining room. His two principal lodge jobs were running the dining room and keeping the books. I didn't normally see him until breakfast time because he used to first get the bank deposits and previous day's receipts balanced or tied out.

In the dining room, he had two goals: to make sure that everything was going well and that everyone had a full glass of cool, clear water at every table, and, as the principal public relations person, to talk to anyone who would listen to him about the Badlands and the need to protect this resource. He customarily carried a pitcher of ice water to tables as his way of introducing himself and then happily answered any and all questions.

Every evening after dinner, grandfather continued educating people about the Badlands with his most important daily ritual. As the temperature cooled and the sky cleared, most guests enjoyed sitting outside on the terrace. There, grandfather would give lectures and answer questions about the Badlands. At dusk he would show the guests movies with a projector. For several years there was no ranger or park office on site. Grandfather acted as the principal information source about the Badlands. He had a captive audience and the guests seemed to love it. He continued this interactive presentation until the year of his death in 1956. These lectures were such an impressive ceremony that the tradition of guests sitting outside in front of the lodge continued after his death.

What's fascinating is that the beginning of the space age and the introduction of satellites attracted even more guests to join the group on the terrace. The sky was so clear and the temperature so agreeable that people would sit for hours watching the satellites. It's almost as if the Russians had planned to initiate their first dog in space, Laika, the year after grandfather died. The international sensation watching Laika overhead was that you could imagine the sound as it passed to be "**beep beep bow wow**."

In those days, the original dining room was down the stairs off the gift shop and had approximately twelve tables, seating about fifty people. Although the dining room was on the lowest level, the basement level, there were several advantages to it. Because the dining room was belowground, it maintained a very moderate temperature. Although there was no air conditioning, a fan moved the air to keep it comfortable and, in midday, much cooler than outside. The room was cozy, resembling a high-end cabin's interior, with a family atmosphere. The walls were cedar, and the air was infused with a mild pine smell.

Later, in the 1950s, as Grandfather aged, some of the longtime waitresses would tell me how they were terrified that he might spill the water. But after years of practice, I guess he was steadier than he looked and he only had minor essential tremors. The waitresses told me that he was a "real bear" in the dining room in insisting that the place looked good, the service was professional, and the food was tasty.

The dining room was recounted as a hallmark of the place. Grandfather and Uncle Herb insisted from the beginning on a full-course menu each day, which meant choice cuts of meats with properly cooked potatoes and various other vegetables. Good iced tea and coffee were also important. No skimping on quality or trying to stretch the time over which it could be kept heated was allowed, and there was no reheating. Coffee was routinely thrown out and a fresh batch made if it was deemed "over the hill." There had to also be a tempting menu for young cowpokes traveling with their families, complete with fresh homemade pies, cakes, and fruit dishes. Each morning, our family would meet with the chef and plan the next day's menu. The details had to be discussed and agreed upon, making sure all the correct supplies were on hand or that it was certain they could be obtained later in the day. The agreed-upon menu was typed up, and copies were made and given to the dining room staff for the next day's diners and to the upstairs gift shop crew so they could answer visitors' inquiries. Copies of the menu were kept on the long table at which the employees had their meals so that everyone working had a chance to look the menu over.

Obtaining and storing the premium quality products for the dining room was a big undertaking. The lodge had two walk-in units. The refrigerated unit contained fresh vegetables, milk, juices, and fruits. The walk-in freezer unit was for meats, fish, ice cream, and ice. Keeping these units fully stocked was the chef's job. He could rely on regular food-delivery trucks, such as Schwan's food-delivery service,[31] for emergency small packages or refrigerated items. As far as the larger items, such as sides of beef, lamb or pork, Grandfather and I drove all the way to Chamberlain. Some vegetables could be ordered for delivery on the daily train at the stop in Interior. Once or possibly twice a week, Uncle Herb and I would go to Rapid City and visit Safeway or another large grocery.

---

[31] South Dakota Schwan trucks maintained a regular, timely delivery service, and Cedar Pass Lodge was a continuing good customer, especially for necessary, small, or forgotten items.

One day, the famous author of travel books, reviewing lodgings and restaurants, Duncan Hines of Chicago, arrived unannounced. He booked a cabin and stayed for a couple days, marveling at what he had discovered. Of course, Grandfather and Uncle Herb took Duncan Hines to see all the facilities and explained how, and from how far away, the ingredients came. Duncan Hines took it all in, including the minutia and the macro details of the operation. I always thought the pièce de résistance of his two-day visit might have been the attention to detail he experienced—in the form of nice sheets—in his Cedar Pass Lodge cabin. Aunt Faye lived in Chicago and frequented Marshall Field & Company stores and knew their products well. Neno would call occasionally and ask if Faye could locate something they needed, often something for the cabins (probably linens). Faye would send them a package with very nice sheets, pillowcases, and so on, as a gift. There was a giant difference in the feel and look of Marshall Field's better-grade linens. When my wife and I were staying at Cedar Pass for a few days, Patty was amazed at the linens in the cabins and used to joke with Aunt Faye about her job as a "contract forager and buyer" for Cedar Pass Lodge.

Duncan Hines was effusive in his compliments to Grandfather and Grandmother. He was impressed with the operation at Cedar Pass Lodge, writing glowing reports in his travel articles. The word spread quickly. New guests started citing Duncan Hines's endorsement as their reason to visit. Sophisticated travelers from Chicago poured in.

On several occasions over the years, I interviewed members of the Hustead family of Wall Drug Store fame. They commented, "Your grandfather and Uncle Herb showed us how to run a really first-class operation."

Dewey Beard and Alice at Cedar Pass Lodge

Back in 1936, when my sister Glenna and I made our first trip to the Badlands, the first thing we saw through the windows of Dad's car that caught our attention and stuck with us was Dewey and Alice Beard's white tepee.

I don't even have to imagine what thousands and thousands of kids making a similar trip said as their car came down the hill called Cedar Pass. They said exactly what Glenna or I said: "Oh, look, there's an Indian tepee down there!"

Beginning back then, and for years and years in the 1940s, Dewey had made some kind of an arrangement (well, Alice probably was the "arranger") with Grandfather or Grandmother to come and set up their tepee in the front of the lodge near the road. Grandfather and Grandmother provided Dewey and Alice with a small, basic cabin to sleep in and to store their personal items each summer season.

Every day, starting early, Dewey dressed in his usual "dress clothes" for picture taking, wearing an eagle feather headdress, moccasins, and the works. He would pose for tourists while they took either still photos or movie films of him as he chanted or sang a bit, doing a short dance. Alice would collect the money from the tourists.

I know that Alice and Grandmother had an unofficial arrangement whereby Grandmother would often get some food from the kitchen or have Joe, the chef, put together a little plate for them.

What I do not know, and it would be difficult if not impossible to find out, is when and where Grandfather first met Dewey in person. Reasonable speculations would suggest that it may have been shortly after Grandfather arrived in the Badlands and started work on building Cedar Pass Lodge. Perhaps their first meeting occurred during the time Grandfather and his sister Clara were operating the dance hall that Clara had built. That speculation is reasonable because they likely employed either full-time or part-time Native American help from the Pine Ridge Indian Reservation just across the White River, less than a mile away.

Although not much material is available detailing the substantial number of years that Dewey and Alice spent their summers at Cedar Pass Lodge, fortunately, on our first family trip to visit Grandfather and family in 1936, my father, who was an avid photographer, brought along his crank-up 16 mm movie camera with color film in it. During his many years at Ruskin Park, his experience with moviemaking culminated with the founding of a traveling motion picture studio. Dad even brought a movie production consultant from California to Ruskin Park. As a result, he had access to early forms of color movie film. He shot a number of feet in color film of Cedar Pass Lodge and specifically Dewey and Alice Beard.[32]

During my time as cabin boy in the 1940s, and after that in the early 1950s, several times a day when the tourist traffic was slow, I would spend a few minutes with Dewey and Alice. Dewey taught me to count to ten in Sioux, which I still remember, although until the Internet arrived, I could only review it vocally.[33]

---

[32] I donated these films to the Institute of Historical Survey based in Las Cruces, New Mexico, along with many other films and records.

[33] For the heck of it, I went on Google and asked for the translation. Amazingly, the numbers for two, three, and four are much like what is still in my head seventy-three years later. In the Sioux language, numbers two, three,

Dewey also gave me an eagle feather headdress, a tomahawk, and a pair of slippers over the years. As a teenager, I didn't realize their value, and I gave them to Ozzie Klavestad, I believe his name was, who ran the Stagecoach Bar & Grill near Shakopee, Minnesota, which closed several years ago. I had been so impressed with his collection of western memorabilia, and when we moved, I had to cut back on my collections, so I thought of him. My training as a pack rat, after years with Grandmother, was firmly established. I was convinced, however, that my hoard of items was multiplying at night.

In the mid-1940s, after I had received my driver's license from Minnesota, I often drove Uncle Herb out to the Pine Ridge Indian Reservation to pick up a new employee that he had hired. I knew firsthand that Grandfather had gone to the reservation to interview and meet people who later worked for many years at Cedar Pass Lodge.

You might be wondering how Grandfather, his sister Clara, Uncle Herb, and others, found employees on the reservation who had the background or experience to work at the lodge.[34] A couple of people, at a minimum, who were close friends of our family had immediate connections to the reservation. For example, Louie Herscher and his wife Annabell owned property on the reservation and farmed it. Louie was one of a kind, and my wife Patty and I, with Uncle Herb, loved to engage him in long detailed discussions over dinners or whenever we had a chance to see each other. It was obvious to me that there was a bond between Louie and Grandfather. You could immediately see it whenever they met each other.

---

and four are *Nu'NPA*, *YA'mni*, and *TO'PA*. In my vocal remembrance, I would have said *Nupa*, *Yamini*, and *Dopa*. (Dakota and Lakota are Siouan languages of the Great Plains.)

[34] I happened to think of this as the "grapevine" or informal organization, which was the area in which I wrote my PhD thesis for my degree at the University of Minnesota in 1968.

In the last few years of Grandfather's life, in the mid-1950s, (he left us in 1956 for another planet), I used to travel out to the Badlands with my hunting dog. Once, in the fall, during the season for hunting sharp-tailed grouse, I asked Uncle Herb if he had any ideas of where I might go hunting. Right away, he suggested consulting Louie. Louie was all for the idea and suggested that maybe Grandfather might like to go along to watch. Grandfather, I knew, had done a lot of bird hunting in the past, so off we went. I could tell he was really looking forward to a break in his daily routine.

To shorten the story to the basics, my dog was a very good English Setter with lots of experience. Grandfather and Louie sat down on a ridge, below which was a harvested wheat field with some nice "bluffs" as we called the small bunches of trees or low brush in which, during midday, the grouse go to get out of the sun and seek protection from hawks.

My dog, Riddum, knew what he was doing, but I wanted to make sure Grandfather got to see some grouse. As a result, I was hollering too many instructions to the dog. After a bit, Louie stood up and hollered at me, "George, will you shut up and let the dog do his thing. He knows more about it than you, and if you'd shut your damn mouth, maybe we'd get some dinner if you can hit anything with that double barrel you are carrying around." Grandfather was laughing and enjoying the whole show.

A few minutes later, Riddum pointed to a nice covey, and I managed to get dinner for all of us. It was a great fall day, perfect weather for hunting, and the company couldn't have been better.

Louie Herscher with Riddum at his ranch on the
Pine Ridge Sioux Reservation, 1956.

Of course, Louie had lots of friends on the reservation. He was a great reference source. Being a

hardworking rancher who refused to use new, fancy motorized machinery, he insisted on

plowing, cultivating, and harvesting with his teams of animals. This made him all the more

interesting in long, relaxed conversations.

Beyond that, several members of the Cedar Pass Lodge staff either lived on the reservation or

had friends there. Among them, was Willard Sharp, a longtime maintenance guy. People in

Interior also employed folks from the reservation and recommended reliable residents looking

for work.

It would be a mistake not to include a relatively short description of the years 1890 to 1942,

which were nearly unbelievably terrible for Dewey and his family. The accounts include not only

what happened to them at the Massacre of Wounded Knee in South Dakota, but also later, at the beginning of World War II, when the government confiscated Dewey's land to use as a bombing range. They didn't receive nearly enough in compensation to live on.

Iron Hail joined the Ghost Dance movement and was in Spotted Elk's band along with his parents, siblings, wife and child. He and his family left the Cheyenne River Indian Reservation on December 23, 1890 with Spotted Elk and approximately 300 other Miniconjou and 38 Hunkpapa Lakota on a winter trek to the Pine Ridge Indian Reservation to avoid the perceived trouble which was anticipated in the wake of Sitting Bull's murder at Standing Rock Indian Reservation. He and his family were present at the Wounded Knee Massacre, where he was shot three times, twice in the back, and some of his family, including his mother, father, wife and infant child were killed. He recounted his experiences in an in-depth interview with Eli S. Ricker for a book Ricker planned to write.

Dewey Beard changed his name from Iron Hail when he converted to Roman Catholicism. He was a member of Buffalo Bill's Wild West Show for 15 years.

In the early 1940s Beard and his wife Alice were raising horses on their land on the Pine Ridge Indian Reservation. In 1942 the Department of War annexed 341,725 acres (138,291 ha) of the reservation for use as an aerial gunnery and bombing range. Beard's family was among the 125 Lakota families uprooted from their homes. They were compensated by the government for their land in installments which were too low to enable them to afford more property, and as a result they both moved into a poor section of Rapid City.

When he died in 1955 at the age of ninety-six, Dewey Beard was the last known Lakota survivor of the **Battle of the Little Bighorn**, and the last known Lakota survivor of the Wounded Knee Massacre. (Dewey Beard, n.d.)

At Cedar Pass
1936

Dewey Beard/Iron Hail/Wasú Ma'za.

It is curious to speculate about how the friendship developed between Dewey Beard and Grandfather after they first met, whenever that was, but there was obviously a mutual understanding between Dewey and Alice and our family.

What I noticed about Cedar Pass Lodge, whose tone was set by Grandfather, Grandmother Uncle Herb, and Aunt Dorothy, was that they recognized the mutual benefit of Dewey and Alice's presence. Their tepee was right in front of them every day during the season. I saw and heard how all of them referred to Dewey and Alice, and I never recall hearing anyone in the family speak degradingly about them. Neno, on a daily basis, brought Dewey and Alice snacks or got them plates of food. Certainly, Joe the chef, Uncle Herb, Aunt Dorothy, and then Grandfather indirectly, if not directly, must have seen and known all about the arrangement.

Alice was strong willed, but that was justified and understood. It was not an easy life for Dewey and Alice.

Native dancers at the fiftieth anniversary of the founding of Badlands National Park.

Native dancers also at the fiftieth anniversary.

Field Trips

Time off with Uncle Herb was the high point of any day. During the off-seasons, way into the 1950s and 1960s, before and after Grandfather's death in 1956, I was able to spend time at Cedar Pass with Grandmother and Aunt Dorothy. Patty and I moved to Huron, South Dakota, and later to Denver, Colorado. On long weekends or vacations, we usually spent time at Cedar Pass. The field trips involved participating in activities Uncle Herb enjoyed and in which he had become quite proficient. He had learned and studied over the years not only photography but also developing and printing his own films and making enlargements. In addition, he had spent hundreds of days hunting for agates, petrified wood, jasper, and fossils, in part to supply his own lapidary shop. Uncle Herb had become very knowledgeable in lapidary science.

Patty Millard "photographer" with her Minox Camera
in the Badlands on South Dakota, 1956.

In effect, these activities are a brief, partial answer to the question of, "Why visit the Badlands?" Beyond those hunting for treasures, there is a whole additional group of activities outlined in the NPS brochures on the Badlands, including bird-watching (or "birding"), searching for prairie flowers and plants, and viewing animals. In the past several years, there has been a dramatic increase in the variety of animals reintroduced to the Badlands, such as the Rocky Montain bighorn sheep and the black-footed ferret.

When visiting Cedar Pass in the past few years, stopping at the first overlook on entering the park from the east, I've been astonished to see bighorn sheep. They calmly munch on buffalo grass along the road or the edge of the parking lot. Bighorn sheep, buffalo, and other animals had been previously eliminated from the Badlands. Other species of animals reintroduced by the NPS programs have also been very successful. Buffalos were the first animals reintroduced in 1963, and the park estimates there are about 800 now. Another species of animal under the reintroduction program is the black-footed ferret:

> This small, nocturnal weasel made its home within the vast prairie dog towns of the west and fed on their residents. As ranches replaced prairie dog towns, the ferrets' population dwindled. In 1987, only 18 individuals remained, living on a remote Wyoming ranch. As one of the most endangered land mammals in the world, a captive breeding program was quickly begun. By 1992, ferrets were being released back into the wild and were returned to the Badlands just two years later. The current population has rebounded to approximately 300 through the Conata Basin and Badlands area administered by the National Park Service and U.S. Forest Service. (Dakota, n.d.)

Visitors today may catch a glimpse of animals missing from the area for decades. The swift fox was also successfully reintroduced:

Populations of this small native fox declined due to mortalities from predator control, targeted at wolves and coyotes. This species is our park's newest restoration project, returned in the fall of 2004 after a hiatus of over 40 years. The population is now estimated at 60 to 80 individuals and will be augmented in the upcoming years. The largest percentage now lives in the Buffalo Gap National Grassland surrounding the park, successfully raising new pups. (Dakota, n.d.)

Future Spending Habits of the Modern Tourists Herald Change

Due to the cell phones and digital cameras not requiring film, the bottom has really dropped out of one of the previous big moneymakers—camera film—for Cedar Pass Lodge's store as well as for thousands of other convenience stores around the country.

However, entirely new, ever-expanding categories of convenience store items are multiplying the dollar sales several times over. Self-serve beverage bars, "roller-heated" foods on hot bars, prepackaged sandwiches, single-serve drinks in cans and bottles or boxes, and cell phone accessories are just some examples

Since my first trip to the Badlands in 1936, progress in the field of refrigeration has changed the car tourism experience and the retail operations that cater to it. Where Cedar Pass and others depended on swamp coolers, there is now air conditioning and refrigerators everywhere. Travelers have portable foam ice chests or even a Coleman cooler plugged into their car.

Simple changes like these in spending by future park visitors will push the NPS to rethink the use of their limited available facilities, including Cedar Pass Lodge. It appears that a lower percentage of tourists are getting off the paved roads. They enjoy the vistas from the new scenic paved road and grab a quick snack. The service demands of guests may see the lodge turn into something entirely new.

Badlands Geological Formations: Uniquely Picturesque, Valuable for Study, and Not Found Elsewhere

So, to conclude this chapter, I'd like to share a personal experience at Cedar Pass back in the 1940s. At certain times of the day, there was often a lull in the customer counts to the lodge store. I figured that I could help, based on my hunting experiences by setting out some "decoys" in front of the lodge by the highway. So, I'd go and drive various cars and pickups to the front mimicking a bustling parking lot. One day, while I was doing just that, a very strange looking bus, unusually large and oddly shaped, came down the Millard Ridge hill and drove into our parking area. The doors opened and all of the passengers streamed out straight into the lodge. I knew they were not from the United States, as I heard them speaking. I wagered they were from a Scandinavian country. I started talking to the driver and found out they were, in fact, Scandinavian. The bus was a Scandinavian tour bus from their own country that they had brought over on the ship with them. The driver said that the South Dakota Badlands was their first scheduled stop and therefore an important one. I asked him why that was, and he told me, "Well, just look around. Your Badlands are one of the very best places in the world to observe and learn, from geology, how our world has come to be what it is."

In other words, Senator Norbeck's statement when he submitted the proposal for protection of the Badlands was spot on.

> Whereas there is a small section of country about the headwaters of the White River in South Dakota where Nature has carved the surface of the earth into most unique and interesting forms, and has exposed there, in the geological formations to an extent, perhaps not elsewhere found; and

> Whereas this formation is so unique, picturesque, and valuable for the purposed of study that a portion should be retained in its native state. (Bahr, Vermeer, & Haecker Architects, Ltd., in association with John Milner Associates, Inc., and Renewable Technologies, Inc., 2006, p. 233)

Chapter 11: The Progressive View Must Continue!

George Millard holding Ben Millard's rifle and powder horn. Donated to the Badlands National Park in 2016.

One day, some twenty-eight years ago, I received a call out of the blue from Fred Thomas, a reporter from the Omaha (Nebraska) *Sunday World-Herald* newspaper. I don't know how he got my name, and I had no idea what the purpose of the call was. He asked me if I was the grandson of Ben H. Millard.

I replied that I was. Thomas said he was writing a column called "Your Environment," for the June 17th, 1990, Sunday edition. The article concerned vacation time and his suggestions as to how and where vacationers might choose to spend their vacation time. He asked if he might ask

166

me a few questions about my grandfather, Ben H. Millard, some of my impressions about the Badlands National Park, and my experiences there.

Although I've been working on this book for several years, at the time of Thomas's phone call I had not even considered it. However, I began to consider, toward the end of this project, if any of my comments for his article still hold water. Additionally, what conclusions could be drawn regarding the vision and plans Grandfather and Senator Norbeck had insisted on as they worked and struggled to see the Badlands National Park established. Both of these men passed away before the Badlands National Park was established. Maybe it would have been established anyway, but I doubted that to be true for reasons I mentioned to Thomas.

The article was titled, "Book, Views of Plains Depicts Its Strength," in which Thomas provides a background to an extensive and thorough study referred to several places in this book that was done for the NPS just twelve years ago. That study answers some of the questions brought up in this article.

The article begins as follows:

> When vacation time comes, some residents of the prairies and plains feel an inferiority complex. Living without mountains and seashores, they don't think of their surroundings as the place many tourists go. Two more ways are available to offset that feeling.
>
> One is a new book, the "Smithsonian Guide to Historic America: The Plains States." The other is the view of plainsman, George Millard.

The Smithsonian guide is a beautifully illustrated 461 page look at 6 states—Missouri, Kansas, Nebraska, Iowa and the Dakotas—and how they evolved.

In the introduction, Roger Kennedy, Director of the National Museum of American History, offers a range of comments. Two samples:

"Despite cities, despite office parks and manufacturers of computer chips, despite vineyards and orchards, the dominant element of the Missouri Valley remains water and grass."

The "glory of the natural Nebraska is the Sandhills Region . . . nearly 10 thousand square miles in extent. Here are the lakes and grassy plains as they were when the first humans came upon the scene. . . . Here the High Plains can be seen as they were when the Oregon Trail was crawling with westering Americans. Travelers today who come in search of peace can cross those vestiges of primitive America, as grand in their understated way as the Wind River Range or the Tetons."

More Comfortable [Thomas's final section]:

[George] Millard, a Minnesotan with Nebraska and South Dakota connections, said plains residents are gaining new respect for their land and heritage, and tourists are coming in increasing numbers. Once shy about their surroundings, plains residents now are extolling them, he said.

In an interview, Millard recalled people who couldn't wait to move out of the Prairie and didn't think it had the lure for people who grew up in the mountains or along seashores.

"A national park, many felt, must be grand and awe-inspiring scenery which would impress our European forefathers—a Glacier or the Tetons," he said. "Now we all feel more comfortable about the Prairie" and its attractions, he said.

Thanks to Garrison Keillor's "Prairie Home Companion" radio show, authors and others, the Prairie has become better understood and appreciated, Millard said.

A resident of St. Paul Minn., Millard offers an admittedly prejudiced view. His grandfather, former Nebraskan, Ben Millard, was a leader in establishing Badlands National Park in South Dakota.

The effort took years—kind of like the effort it is taken to have people appreciate the plains and the prairies, and to find relaxation in them. [The Badlands] offers steep canyons, gullies, ridges, spires and knobs and grasslands and the animals that live in such areas from pronghorns and prairie dogs to bison and bighorn sheep.

"The Badlands is a great attraction, not only because the scenery is spectacular, but also because it protects so many prairie plants, animals and wonders, not to mention the geology and fossils so prevalent there," [George] Millard said. Ben Millard, born in Minnesota, moved as a young man to Decatur, Neb., worked on a Missouri River ferry and as a cowhand, and attended school in Lincoln, Neb.

He wound up in South Dakota as the agent of Peter Norbeck, the US senator who pushed for preserving the Badlands as a National Monument. Like Norbeck, Ben Millard and others had the vision to understand the value of the Badlands ecological system, George Millard said.

The Millards operated the Cedar Pass Lodge, near Interior, S.D., within the Badlands.

George Millard said his grandfather was one of the people who convinced federal officials that the natural values of the Badlands made it important enough to become a national monument.

[Ben] Millard's role in creating a Badlands National Monument is chronicled in a book, "A Revelation Called the Badlands," published by the Badlands Natural History Association last year on the 50th anniversary of the establishment of the monument.

Herbert Millard, Ben's son, helped develop Cedar Pass Lodge. (Thomas, 1990)

To balance this article because, as Thomas pointed out, my comments admittedly offered a prejudiced view, I offer the following study commissioned by NPS and completed in 2006. The "Milner Report"depicts the huge increased wave of tourists annually visiting national parks and the reasons such a wave was created. As Thomas's article points out, a significant catalyst in the wave was the change in attitude on the part of the public to take advantage of the splendor of our national park resources, especially in the younger generations of our society.

A corollary to these observations by Thomas's article, and the conclusions of the "Milner Report", are the vast changes cited in the previous chapter of this book. Now, with the omnipresent convenience stores and their incredible array of chilled bottle drinks, ready-made sandwiches, and hot food items (hot dogs, pizza, hamburgers, tacos, etc.), once again, the NPS is faced with updating park facilities, camping areas, and outdoor activities.

Then, an updated strategy of how to approach the new lifestyles of the times under the NPS "Mission 66" program began in 1955:

> Ten years after the end of World War II, economic prosperity catapulted Americans into a lifestyle that had greater flexibility, wealth, mobility, and opportunities for recreation. This new lifestyle prompted visitation at state and national parks to rise to record numbers. In 1955, the number of visitors to national parks totaled 50 million, twice the number that the parks were equipped to accommodate. A strategy for how to address this issue became of paramount importance to the NPS. Mission 66 was a ten-year program in which Congress authorized a financial package that would support development in the National Parks, bringing them up to twentieth-century standards by the fiftieth anniversary of the creation of the National Park Service in 1966. (Bahr, Vermeer, & Haecker Architects, Ltd., in association with John Milner Associates, Inc., and Renewable Technologies, Inc., 2006, p. 247)

Even before national park status was granted to the Badlands, the number of visits had climbed:

In September 1954, 15-1/2 years after the national monument was established, the five millionth visit was recorded. A total of ten million visits was attained just seven years later in July 1961. On August 16, 1966, Superintendent Frank A. Hjort officially welcomed a traveler and his family who represented the 15 millionth visit to Badlands National Monument. (Mattison & Grom, 1968, p. 65)

A much broader question is whether Senator Norbeck and Ben's vision and foresight in seeking national monument and national park protection for the Badlands carried beyond the Badlands to other areas, new or being remodeled, as the Badlands developments were over the years.

Recognizing the Historic Significance of Badlands National Park (1993–2006)

Research into the historic significance of various aspects of Badlands National Park has been undertaken primarily in the developed area of Cedar Pass. Individual resources that have been evaluated and found eligible for their significance include the Cedar Pass Road, the Cedar Pass to Northwest Entrance Road, and the Ben Reifel Visitor Center. In addition, a recent Cultural Landscape Report (CLR) prepared by John Milner Associates in 2005, found the Cedar Pass Developed Area to be eligible for listing in the National Register under Criteria C in the area of planning. The South Dakota State Historic Preservation Office (SDSHPO) concurred with the findings of the CLR. (Bahr, Vermeer, & Haecker Architects, Ltd., in association with John Milner Associates, Inc., and Renewable Technologies, Inc., 2006, p. 256)

The Milner Report's final conclusions, with concurrence from the SDSHPO, are given at the end of the report:

The Cedar Pass landscape is a complex of resources, including the lodge and cabins, the two campgrounds, the Visitor Center and parking, the seasonal and single-family residences, the maintenance area, and the roads within the Cedar Pass Developed Area. Together these resources can be understood as an expression of Mission 66 planning concepts, which were intended to achieve the following:

- improve access by developing interpretive facilities as close to the resource as possible;

- expand interpretive opportunities by extending interpretation into the landscape through a range of experiential activities;

- establish synergies between educational programs and signature park resources;

- use curvilinear forms to allow for multiple views and an unimpeded processional;

- manage visitor movement;

- cluster relatively dense site planning of new facilities and complexes;

- utilize a unifying design concept that made use of an armature or datum along which development occurred;

- employ zoning of like uses;

- practice the visual and physical separation of different uses;

- avoid fragile resources in site developments;

- incorporate existing features into new designs; and

- espouse the use of modern materials and construction methods and minimizing of detailing and ornamentation in order to avoid distraction from the surrounding natural or historic resource.

As such the Cedar Pass Developed area is considered eligible for listing in the National Register under Criterion C. . . . In addition, it is likely that future research will find other, both surface and subsurface, resources within the Badlands National Park, that are eligible for listing in the National Register for their association with attempts to create a tourist attraction, conserve a nationally significant place of profound scenic and scientific value, and create a National Park.

National Park status for the Badlands was achieved after a long process and the determined efforts of a few individuals. Development progressed slowly, but proved to be sensitive to the natural resources, while concurrently offering greater numbers of visitor services and facilities. In the process of developing a National Park, a valuable resource was protected and preserved. (Bahr, Vermeer, & Haecker Architects, Ltd., in association with John Milner Associates, Inc., and Renewable Technologies, Inc., 2006, pp. 257-258)

My recommendations are not very scientific, but for my two cents, I'd say we all need to visit the national parks and monuments and soak up the years of good vibes in the long-standing buildings. It's a great pleasure to stand in Yellowstone National Park's Old Faithful Lodge and just be awed by the timbers and wood. Similarly, those huge logs that Grandfather trucked down from the Black Hills, stripped, and used for bracing the ceiling, and those they split lengthwise and cut to make the steps down to the "basement" where the old dining room used to be, still give me pleasure just to see them.

And, finally, we must not allow short-term pressures to dictate digging, drilling, fracking, mining, and so on, in areas previously protected. As time has gone by, the foresight and vision of protecting unique lands as national treasures has increasingly been validated. President Theodore Roosevelt (republican) and President Franklin D. Roosevelt (democrat), two of our strongest conservation-minded presidents, set aside land areas in protected status. The value of those lands has dramatically increased, judging by the number of our residents who make use of them.

Acknowledgments

Grandfather Ben's early experiences were as a small-town South Dakota banker. In the banking tradition, over eighty years ago, I started my trust account of notes, names, nomenclature, and necessary notations. I didn't know what purpose my Badlands Information Trust (BIT) account papers were going to serve. As a qualified pack rat, I squirreled them away along with agate fossil pieces and rattlesnake rattles from the Badlands. Unfortunately, papers and notes don't have the same resilience over time that rocks and minerals do, so some are lost due to humidity or mold. The rocks are still fine and should last another 250,000 years by my estimates.

The following list of acknowledgments starts back eighty years ago and is not in chronological order (please excuse unintended errors, should your name be missing):

The long, long hours of conversations with Uncle Herbert Millard, Grandmother (Neno), and Aunt Faye Millard MacFarland are still my constant companions. Strange as it may appear, I didn't hear as much from my father as I heard from them. Of course, I spent many days and years later with them after Grandfather died in 1956.

After the sale of Cedar Pass Lodge to the government in 1963, Uncle Herb and Aunt Dorothy left South Dakota and moved to a ranch south of Livingston, Montana. There, at times, we had long discussions about days in the Badlands and Grandfather, where I picked up a lot more information. Somewhat later, when I was Marshall Fields' Commissionaire Agent for South America, I had business in Chicago that often found me staying at Aunt Faye's apartment and learning more of Grandfather's history.

Keith Crew, my longtime rancher friend who owns the ranch property just outside the east entrance to the park, has put up with me during all the times I worked, stayed, and visited Cedar Pass. Keith's mother and father were as close to Grandfather, Grandmother, Uncle Herb, and Aunt Dorothy as anyone in the Badlands. We frequently had lunches, coffee, or dinner together and would get to talking about some road problem or cattle problem or whatever piece of information had relevance in some way to history. I'd scribble down a few notes and save them.

For going on twenty years, I've been working with, visiting, and donating materials to the Institute of Historical Survey Foundation (IHSF) in Las Cruces, New Mexico, where a substantial number of Cedar Pass Lodge and Badlands clippings about Grandfather are now in their files, as well as all sorts of photographs, slides, and other materials from Ruskin Park and the Badlands. Dr. Evan Davies, the president of the institute, and particularly Richard Layne, the head of the audiovisual department, are perhaps the strongest reasons that I have continued to work on this book. They encouraged me to press on with researching sources and putting together materials to be able to eventually get down to writing.

Richard Layne's assistance and advice in researching old newspapers has been invaluable. He also digitized my extensive collection of tape-recorded interviews and many slides and photographs and then supplied me with easy-to-use copies. I also would be remiss if I were not to mention Anne Morgan and her staff, including Hanna Moulder and other great people working at IHSF in New Mexico. They catalog the materials that I donate and have been exceedingly helpful in retrieving parts needed to write the book.

My father, Glen Millard "Dad" became interested in filming due to early work in setting up a traveling motion picture studio at Ruskin Park, South Dakota, in the late 1920s with a writer and technician from Hollywood, California. In 1935, he had access to some very early color, 16 mm film. In 1936, he used it to film my mother, my sister Glenna, Grandmother, and me, including several feet of footage of the famous Sioux Indian chief, Dewey Beard, and his wife Alice at Grandfather Ben's Cedar Pass Lodge in the Badlands of South Dakota. It's a real treasure and fun to watch.

As I write the last few pages of this book, I feel I should refer to Josh Whitaker as my co-researcher and writer. There is absolutely no doubt in my mind that without Josh's help and patience, I would never have finished this book. For several weeks on end, we worked from 9:00 am until late at night, seven days a week, on the computer or digging through the papers and files.

Ben and Helen Zoss in South Dakota proved another principle source of support, with incredibly knowledgeable and well-researched information. Ben and Helen are the owners of the previous Ruskin Park property near Forestburg, South Dakota. Ben opened his doors and provided information on the chain of title in land holdings of Grandfather and others of Ruskin Park.

Richard Varco, my close hunting friend and a former senior member of the Minnesota Attorney General's Office for thirty-six years or so, traveled with me to South Dakota for three or four days as the audiovisual expert in interviews with Ben Zoss. We taped well over one hundred pages of notes on my discussions with Zoss that were later typed by IHSF.

Back in 2015, I had been trying to find information about our family's close friend, Chuck Orelup of Rapid City, South Dakota, who owned Rise Studio and was the producer of most of the postcards sold at Cedar Pass Lodge. I struck out on the search. However, in the phone book, I found his son, Robert Orelup, and had one of the nicest, short interviews of my quest for firsthand accounts. I would like to thank Robert here and acknowledge the gift of letters he had saved. These letters between Chuck, Grandfather, Grandmother, and Uncle Herb give a much clearer picture of the difficult times they experienced.

Recently, three other people have helped me with editing. In particular, I would like to thank Kate Peterson, who was an indispensable, knowledgeable, and technically highly competent assistant. As a student, she had always liked to read and was proficient in English. As a result, I would unconditionally recommend her as an editor, and hope that she decides to enter this field. Graduate English major student Erin Geyen was a great editing help as was Darla Stewart, an RN from near Sioux Falls, South Dakota.

Through all the time of preparing and writing this book, our two sons, Ben Herbert and Stephan Glen, tried to bend their schedules, certainly not intruding on my schedule, to cure computer panics when I did something to upset, aggravate, or confuse my iPad or computers. Stephan is a software person, skilled at setting up and managing marketing programs for software manufacturing companies. Ben works in the software field also, as the intermediary between the unorganized flow of incoming information and the receivers' computers, also known as a "data steward." I thank them for fixing all the panics they have attended. (Just before leaving for New York a couple days ago, Stephan said that if I ever decided to write another book, he was going to sail his boat to the Caribbean but leave no forwarding address.)

At times, admittedly, I was down in the dumps from fighting the effects of a failed knee replacement over five years and facing a revision of it.[35] My hunting partner and friend since high school, Judge William Canby, helped more than he realized by offering to read and edit some chapters of this book. In addition, two other longtime hunting and fishing friends, Richard Varco (mentioned above) and Rodney Sando, former Department of Natural Resources (DNR) Commissioner in Minnesota for eight years and then DNR Commissioner in Idaho, offered to edit some parts of the book as they had done on my other book about our family's adventures in Peru and Uruguay when I served as US Peace Corps country director during the late 1960s and early 1970s.

---

[35] (Every so often some motion or activity would cause me to be in excruciating pain and unable to walk with crutches or any cane for even two or three steps. This condition made writing difficult as sitting at the computer was next to the worst thing I could do was sit in a chair for any period.)

My shirttail relative, Nick McNeely, a lawyer and legislative consultant, also provided editing support to help me get through last fall.

My dog Luna, who stood in for me during my hunting trips since I couldn't walk more than a few yards, provided me with health, hope, and hunting happiness in spite of all the pressures.

I would like to thank Harry McNeely for his help and assistance during the sale of Cedar Pass Lodge, as well as the McNeely nieces and nephews, especially Shawn and Cara, for their interest and willingness to help on this project.

My sister, Jojo Millard Chervenak, helped edit one of the longer, more complicated chapters and also has been a source of Millard family lore.

Overall, through these recent six years with my unpredictable knee, my greatest support came from another friend of sixty years, former vice president Walter F. Mondale. He kept encouraging me to continue working on the book—as long as it didn't interfere with our fishing trips to Canada and Alaska. At the same time, he insisted that I must pursue answers about my occasionally painful and debilitating leg and knee problem with the Mayo Clinic in Rochester, Minnesota, until they could figure out what had gone wrong with the first knee replacement, which had been performed five years earlier at a different hospital system. So, to prove that he was not about to forget this matter or let it flag on, he had his unbelievably capable and thoughtful assistant, Lynda Pedersen, call Mayo for reports, stressing the urgency of the situation. On top of that, Lynda periodically but consistently called me for updates. (I'm sure Mondale was concerned that I might be late for our 2019 fishing expeditions.) Subsequently, I have submitted an application for Lynda to be named a Saint.

Bibliography

(1919, December 12). *Wallace's Farmer Magazine*, 38. Des Moines, Iowa, United States.

A. G. Becker & Co. (n.d.). Retrieved 2017, from Wikipedia: https://en.wikipedia.org/wiki/A._G._Becker_%26_Co.

Admin. (2013, December 21). "Playground of the Prairie" memorialized with historic marker. *Sanborn Weekly Journal*, p. 11.

Alphabet Agencies. (n.d.). Retrieved from Wikipedia: https://en.wikipedia.org/wiki/Alphabet_agencies

anonymous. (n.d.). Getting Connected. *South Dakota Communities*, 5. Retrieved from https://history.sd.gov/museum/docs/SouthDakotaCommunicates.pdf

Bahr, Vermeer, & Haecker Architects, Ltd., in association with John Milner Associates, Inc., and Renewable Technologies, Inc. (2006). *Discovery and Re-Discovery in the White River Badlands, Historic Resource Study Badlands National Park South Dakota.* National Park Service.

Bradsher, G. (2012). *How the West was Settled, The 150 Year Old Act Lured Americans Looking For A New Life and New Opportunities.* Retrieved from Archives.gov: https://www.archives.gov/files/publications/prologue/2012/winter/homestead.pdf

Centennial Historical Committee. (1982). *Artesian, South Dakota Centennial History 1883-1983.* Woonsocket, South Dakota: Sanborn County Advocate.

Dakota, B. N. (n.d.). *Restoration of Native Animals.* Retrieved from nps.gov/badl/planyourvisit: : https://www.nps.gov/badl/planyourvisit/upload/Wildlife-Reintroductions-Site-Bulletin.pdf

Dewey Beard. (n.d.). Retrieved 2018, from Wikipedia: ttps://en.wikipedia.org/wiki/Dewey_Beard

Dust bowl. (n.d.). Retrieved 2017, from Wikipedia: https://en.wikiedia,org/wiki/Dust_Bowl

Fosness, S. (2018, August 27). Celebrating Norbeck, 'A Pioneer' for South Dakota. *The Daily Republic.*

Go West, young man. (n.d.). Retrieved 2016, from Wikipedia: https://en.wikipedia.org/wiki/Go_West,_young_man

Good Production Was Given. (1915, August 8). *Weekly State Spirit, Huron, SD,.*

History of Taxation in The United States. (n.d.). Retrieved 2017, from Wikipedia: https://en.wikipedia.org/wiki/History_of_taxation_in_the_United_States

Hunter, F. (2010, April 7). *No Ordinary Rabbit: Lewis and Clark Meet "White-Tailed Jack".* Retrieved from Frances Hunter's American Heroes Blog.

JNO Lethem. (1892). Nebraska's Enterprising Cities. In *Historic and Descriptive Review of Nebraska Vol II* (p. 218). Omaha: Lyman & Schmit, General Agents of The Penn Mutual Life Insurance Co of Philadelphia, PA.

Maryott, J. (2005). *Decatur.* Retrieved from The University of Nebraska at Lincoln, Virtual Nebraska: https://casde.unl.edu/history/counties/burt/decatur/index.php

Mattison, R., & Grom, R. (1968). *History of Badlands National Monument and the White River (big) Badlands of South Dakota.* Interior, South Dakota: Badlands Natural History Association.

National Reserve Life Insurance Company. (1956, March 28). A Tribute to Ben Millard (1972-1956). Sioux Falls, South Dakota: Whitmer & Chapman.

Nixon, L. (2015, September 3). *Dakota Life: The Grasshopper and the Plow.* Retrieved from Capital Journal: https://www. Capjournal.com/news/dakota=life-the-grasshopper-and-the plow/article

Online Highways LLC. (2019). *World War II Rationing.* Retrieved from United States History: https://www.u-s-history.com/pages/h1674.html

Pack Rat. (n.d.). Retrieved 2016, from Wikipedia: https://en.wikipedia.org/wiki/Pack_rat

Park, L. D. (1924, August 25th). Labor Day Auto Races at Ruskin Park. *The Mitchelll South Dakota Evening Republican.*

Peter Norbeck. (n.d.). Retrieved 2018, from Wikipedia.

Prairie Homestead. (n.d.). Retrieved 2016, from Wikipedia: https://en.wikipedia.org/wiki/Prairie_Homestead

Rationing. (n.d.). Retrieved 2017, from Wikipedia: https://en.wikipedia.org/wiki/Rationing

Renewable Technologies. (2007). *South Dakota's Railroads: An Historic Context.* Pierre, SD: South Dakota State Historic Preservation Office.

Resettlement Adminstration. (n.d.). Retrieved 2017, from Wikipedia: https://en.wikipedia.org/wiki/Resettlement_Administration

Rosie the Riveter. (n.d.). Retrieved 2016, from Wikipedia: https://en.wikipedia.org/wiki/Rosie_the_Riveter

Ruskin Park Hunting Club. (2015). *Our History.* Retrieved from Ruskinpark.com: http://www.ruskinpark.com/history_2.html

Shuler, J. (1989). *A Revelation Called the Badlands, Building A National Park 1909-1939.* Interior, South Dakota: Badlands Natural History Association.

SWCA Environmental Consultants. (2013). *The History of Agriculture in South Dakota A Fully Developed Historic Context.* South Dakota State Historic Preservation Office.

The Impossible Highway. (n.d.). Retrieved from Visit Rapid City: https://www.visitrapidcity.com/things-to-do/black-hills-cruising/needles-highway

There's a Long Long Trail A-Winding. (n.d.). Retrieved 2017, from Wikipedia: https://en.wikipedia.org/wiki/There%27s_a_Long_Long_Trail_A-Winding

Thomas, F. (1990, June 17). Book, Views of Plains Depict Its Strength. *The Sunday World Herald.*

unknown. (1924, March 14). "Auditorium Is Real Fairyland". *The Huron Evening Huronite.*

unknown. (1924, September 2, September 2). Labor Day Auto Races at Ruskin Park. *The Evening Huronite.*

unknown. (1929). History of Decatur, Nebraska. In unknown, *A History of Burt County, Nebraska from 1903 to 1929* (pp. 1-10). Wahoo: The Ludi Printing Co.

unknown. (1975, March 27). The Story of Ruskin Park. *The Woonsocket News.*

unknown. (1975, May 22). We Called It Decoration Day, Too. *Woonsocket News.*

INDEX

A

A History of Burt County from 1903 to 1929 7
A. G. Granger...100
A. M. Haskell 28, 64
A.G. Becker..114
Aberdeen, South Dakota 27, 75
aerial gunnery and bombing range 161
agate and mineral hunting field trips..............................97
agates 97, 98, 140, 178
agricultural land crisis 105
agricultural land depression..64
Al Smith...104
Albert Jennings...68, 69, 79
Alice Beard 155, 156
Alma Swain..49
alphabet agencies 104, 105
American Academy of Periodontology 115
American Civil War....................................*See US Civil War*
American feminism 137
Anderson Democrat 13
animal viewing 164
Anne Morgan 179
Arlington Hotel 24
army biplanes..37
Artesian High School 44
artesian wells 50
Artesian, South Dakota..3, 25, 115
Attorney General's Office.........................*See Richard Varco*
audiovisual department ....*See Richard Layne*
Auditorium Is Real Fairyland 48
Aunt Dorothy ....*See Dorothy Davis Millard*
avid photographer 156

B

B.H. Millard ....*See Ben Millard*
Bad River 68
Badlands1, 2, 3, 4, 8, 12, 15, 18, 29, 39, 44, 46, 51, 63, 65,
    66, 67, 68, 70, 71, 72, 73, 74, 76, 79, 80, 81, 82, 83, 84,
    85, 86, 87, 88, 89, 90, 91, 92, 93, 94, 95, 97, 98, 99, 100,
    101, 102, 104, 106, 107, 110, 111, 112, 113, 117, 119,
    120, 121, 122, 123, 124,125, 126, 127, 134, 135, 136, 139,
    140, 141, 151, 155, 156, 158, 164, 165, 166, 167, 168,
    169, 171, 172, 173, 174, 175, 176, 178, 179, 180

Badlands National Monument18, 72, 74, 100, 101, 104,
    106, 111, 112, 120, 125, 126, 127, 172, 173
Badlands National Park1, 68, 72, 79, 87, 89, 90, 98, 107,
    141, 168, 169, 171, 174, 175
Badlands National Park Headquarters 87
Badlands Natural History Association 4
Badlands Wall..85, 87
baked-hardpan fields 58
Bank of Interior 68, 89
Battig...42
Battle of the Little Bighorn 161
Bears Ears National Monument 77
Ben Millard 1, 3, 4, 6, 8, 10, 12, 13, 14, 15, 17, 18, 19, 20,
    21, 22, 24, 26, 27, 28, 31, 34, 35, 39, 40, 43, 44, 45, 46,
    48, 49, 57, 58, 63, 65, 66, 67, 71, 77, 78, 81, 82, 83, 85,
    86, 89, 90, 91, 99, 102, 105, 106, 111, 118, 119, 122,
    124, 148, 171, 178, 180, *See Ben Millard*
Ben Millard Stressed Bank Procedure 58
Ben Reifel Visitor Center 86, 174
Ben Zoss 27, 31, 35, 39, 40, 50, 66, 105, 180
bet the farm 18, 92
big bands..38
Bigfoot Pass...85
bighorn sheep...............*See Rocky Mountain bighorn sheep*
Billy, Dale, and Jackie Vitalis...119
bird hunting...158
birding...164
black band ....*See Virginia Ravens*
black blizzards 58, 60
Black Friars ....*See Glen Millard*
Black Hills 69, 72, 75, 76, 79, 85, 89, 92, 134, 139, 176
Black Hills National Bank...18
black rollers 60
Black Sunday 60
Black-footed ferret...164
black-tailed jackrabbit...62
Boise City, Oklahoma 60
bombing range 160
Book, Views of Plains Depicts Its Strength 169
Boundary Waters Canoe Areas Wilderness 77
bowl of alphabet soup 104
Boy ....*See Ben Millard*
Brad Tennant...75
Brakhage 42
Brookings 69
Brookings College..27
Brookings College Hall of Fame.......................................27
Brown family 107
Brownie cameras 134
Budget Office of the Department of the Interior.............83
Buffalo Bill's Wild West Show 160
Buffalo Gap National Grassland 98, 140, 165
buffalo grass..123, 164
Buffalos 164

Bye Painter 130

C

cabin boy 146, 157
California.............................11, 25, 28, 48, 49, 50, 114
Canada...56, 62, 182
Canning, South Dakota 55
Canton, South Dakota 15
Capital Journal 55
car tourism 166
Cara 182
CCC Camp Badlands 126
Cedar Grove ....*See* Juniper Grove
Cedar Pass2, 3, 4, 8, 12, 28, 29, 46, 65, 68, 70, 86, 87, 88,
  89, 90, 91, 92, 93, 94, 95, 96, 98, 100, 103, 111, 112,
  113, 114, 116, 117, 118, 119, 120, 121, 122, 123, 124,
  126, 127, 128, 129, 130, 131, 136, 139, 140, 142, 149,
  153, 154, 155, 156, 157, 159, 161, 163, 164, 165, 166,
  172, 174, 175, 178, 179, 180
Cedar Pass Developed Area 174
Cedar Pass Hotel..................*See* Cedar Pass Lodge
Cedar Pass Lodge2, 3, 4, 8, 12, 28, 29, 46, 65, 68, 87, 88,
  89, 93, 95, 96, 98, 100, 111, 112, 113, 114, 117, 118,
  119, 120, 121, 122, 123, 124, 127, 128, 130, 131, 136,
  140, 142, 153, 154, 155, 156, 157, 159, 161, 165, 166,
  172, 178, 179, 180
Celane No Help Him 143
Chamberlain, South Dakota 88
Champagne Music.....................*See* Lawrence Welk
character of Justice Harkins ....*See* Ben Millard
Charlie's Aunt 50
Chautauqua 27, 32, 33
Chautauqua, New York 32
Cheyenne River Indian Reservation 160
Chicago, Illinois 28, 73, 88, 114, 115, 117, 154, 178
Chief Blackbird 7, 8
Chief Ranger Howard B. Stricklin....................121, 125, 126
Chuck Orelup 131, 132, 133, 134, 135, 180
Civilian Conservation Corps (CCC) 120, 136
Clara Jennings.........................29, 69, 89, 91, 111
Clarence Choos..132
Coe Crawford 71
coincidences 15, 66, 67, 70, 89
color movie film 135, 156
Columbia University 105
combine harvester 59
Commissioner*See* Commissioner of the General Land
  Office
Commissioner of Jackson County..........*See* James Batemen
Commissioner of the General Land Office 88
commodity prices...54
Comptroller-General of the United States....................104
Conata Basin 165

Conata, South Dakota 90
conservation-minded presidents 176
conservative Republicans..............................77
convenience stores 165
Conway Twitty..36
Core of Discovery 61
co-researcher and writer ....*See* Josh Whitaker
Corn Palace 94
Cottonwood State Bank 68
Crystal Lake, Minnesota 93
Cultural Landscape Report (CLR)....................174
Custer State Park 69, 72, 74, 76, 84

D

Dad..................................*See* Glen Millard
daily home-cooked family menu.......................88
Daily Republic..74
Dakota Territory 36, 71
data steward 181
Daum auditorium 48
Decatur Herald 9
Decatur, Nebraska 6, 13
December 20th, 1936.....................................110
Declaration of Independence............................46
Dennis J. Hall 5
Denver, Colorado 139
Department of the Interior 83, 122
Department of War.....................................160
Depression........................54, 56, 99, 106, 114, 115
Depression years 99, 115
Dewey and Alice 155, 156, 162
Dewey Beard.. 8, 10, 139, 143, 155, 156, 157, 160, 161,
  180
Dewey Beard's granddaughter.........................143
Dillon Pass 86
director ....*See* Ruskin Park Plays
Director of Digital Archives 133
Director of the National Museum of American History*See*
  Roger Kennedy
Director of the Park Service 103
Dirty Thirties.......................................54, 59
Dodge special 42
domestic pig bristles 138
dominant element of the Missouri Valley.................170
Don Shaw 52
Donaldson Brothers Flying Circus 37
Dorothy Davis Millard3, 68, 98, 118, 142, 144, 149, 163,
  178, 179
Dowdell...........................24, 26, 27, 35, 44
Dr. Evan Davies 179
Dr. G.W. Mills 100
Dr. Robert E. Pfadt 56
Dresselhuys 42

drought 106
Duisenberg 42
Duncan Hines 154
Dust Bowl years 51, 54, 55, 59

E

eagle feather headdress............................155
East River country....................27, 88, 94, 105
economic prosperity 173
Ed Brown..108
Eddie Rickenbacker 38, 51
Edward Stanley 60
Eli S. Ricker 160
Emergency Relief Administration (ERA).......120
Emin Vitalis 68, 96, 118, 119, 130, 131, 142, 144, 149
environmental degradation 55, 58
Erin Geyen 181
Estella ....*See* Stella Neely Millard
eulogy 3, 17, 18, 28
Evening Huronite 42, 48
Everly Brothers 36
Executive Council 115
Executive Director of the Badlands Natural History
    Association......................*See* Katie Johnston
Executive Order 7027...............................105
executive order, 1922...................................91
exogenous forces 63

F

Fairburn agates 97
Farm Security Administration 105
farmers fed thistles to cattle.........................58
farmland bust..51
fastest dirt track 38, 51
Father of the Badlands 3, 12
Faye......................*See* Faye Millard MacFarland
Faye Millard MacFarland..2, 11, 28, 43, 49, 115, 116, 134,
    140, 154, 178
federal acquisition of private lands...............100
Federal Emergency Relief Administration (FERA) 59
federal income tax 17, 20
Federation Sponsor....................................115
Fedora, South Dakota 26
ferrets..............................*See* black-footed ferret
ferryboat 8
fifteen millionth visit 173
first Badlands interpreter............................111
first native-born governor ....*See* US Senator Peter Norbeck
first personal income tax in 1861.....................19
First State Bank of Phillip 68
First State Bank of Quinn 68
Forestburg, South Dakota 25, 31

former DNR Commissioner......................*See* Rodney Sando
fossil hunting..163
fossils 97, 98, 140, 171
fracking...77, 176
Franconia, Minnesota 118, 119
Frank Lloyd Wright 1
Franklin D. Roosevelt.................104, 105, 119, 176
Fred Thomas 168
frontiersman 109

G

game lodge in Custer State Park 69
Game Sanctuary in the Black Hills...................72
Garden Dance 38
Garrison Keillor 171
Geddes members 74
General Land Office......................................91
geological formations..................................167
George Millard 171, 172
Ghost Dance..160
giant sculpture 71
Glen...*See* Glen Millard
Glen Millard.. 2, 3, 11. 22, 25, 43, 44, 45, 49, 62, 93, 114,
    115, 119, 138, 138, 155, 156
Glenna 93, 94, 96, 155, 179
Go West, young man....................................106
Governor Dennis Daugaard..............................74
Governor Frank Byrne 71
grade school.............................*See* Glen Millard
Grand Tetons National Park 74
Grandfather ....*See* Ben Millard
Grandfather's public schedule 151
Grandmother's private kitchen domain and storage area
   148
Grandmother's secret stash...........................149
Grandpa Boy 149
grandstands..51
grasshopper plague 51, 55, 99
grasshoppers 55, 56, 58, 106, 141
Great Depression.........................51, 54, 55, 104
Great Plains 59, 105, 157
gunnery officer 97

H

H. A. Rodee...27
Hanna Moulder 179
Harriet De Hahn 90
Harry McNeely 182
Harvest Festival 33
Harvest Moon 38
He Fell in Love with His Wife..........................45
head of the audiovisual department........*See* Richard Layne

headquarters residential area 128
Helen Zoss 27, 30, 31, 133
Henry Hewlett 55, 56
Herb ....See Herbert Millard
Herbert Millard.. 3, 18, 43, 49, 64, 68, 77, 94, 95, 96, 97,
   98, 106, 113, 114, 115, 116, 117, 118, 121, 130, 131,
   132, 139, 140, 142, 144, 145, 146, 148, 149, 150, 153,
   154, 155, 157, 158, 161, 163, 172, 178, 179, 180
High Plains 170
Highway 44 ....See State Highway #44
Hiram Augustus "Gus" Rodee 32
History of Decatur, Nebraska 10
Homestead Act 109
homesteader 108, 109
Honolulu Fruit Gum Orchestra ....See Lawrence Welk
Horace Greely 106
Hotsy Totsy Boys ....See Lawrence Welk
House of Representatives 88
Hunkpapa Lakota 160
Hunters Ball 38
Huron Auto Supply Company 26
Huron Light and Power Company 48
Huron Marble and Granite Works......................48
Huron, South Dakota...........................44, 139
Hustead 155

I

Ida Noyes Advisory 115
IHSF ....See Institute of Historical Survey Foundation
Ilo Nelson 92
Indian tepee 155
Indianapolis Speedway...................................42
Institute of Historical Survey Foundation............4, 179, 180
Interior, South Dakota 12, 86, 87, 142, 172
Iowa Normal Monthly 13
Iron Hail...................................See Dewey Beard
Iron Mountain Road 72

J

jackrabbits..61
James Bateman 90
James River...........................15, 27, 30, 32, 33, 52
Japanese surrender in Tokyo Bay......................117
Jay Shuler1, 67, 68, 70, 79, 82, 83, 84, 85, 89, 90, 92, 102,
   110
Joe and Mabel Haight 87
Joe Tlustos......................................31, 40, 133
John McCoy...41, 42
John Milner Associates................................2, 174
John Ruskin...27, 52
Jojo Millard Chervenak................................182
Josh Whitaker...180

Judge William Canby 181
Juniper Grove 91

K

Kadoka, South Dakota..................................88
Kate Peterson..180
Katie Johnston...141
Keith Crew..179
Ken Burns 55
knee replacement 182

L

Labor Day auto races at Ruskin Park, 1924, August 25th..
  42
Lactona....................................115, 138
Lake Crystal, Blue Earth County 6
Lake Superior agates ....See agates
land bust, 1919...27
Land Department 91
lapidary 98, 163
lapidary shop...163
Las Cruces, New Mexico.................................41
last chores of the day...................................144
Lawrence Welk...............................36, 38, 92
Leonel Jensen...100
Leslie and Jessie Crew..................................107
Lester Johnson 142
Lesterville, South Dakota 15, 19
Lewis and Clark...........................7, 9, 61, 62
Lewis and Clark Expedition ....See Lewis and Clark
Lincoln, Nebraska.............12, 14, 15, 16, 21, 66, 118, 171
Lodge ....See Cedar Pass Lodge
Loop Road 1, 84, 85, 86, 87, 93, 94, 103, 108
Lorena Hickok..59
Louie Herscher 158
Louis Foster 49
Louisiana Purchase Exposition 35
Luna...182
Lutheran Seminary 69
Lynda Pedersen 182
Lyons, Nebraska 6

M

Madison County, Indiana 13
Marion C. Dowdell 52
marker #218 (Ruskin Park Marker) 30
married on May 20, 1896.....................See Ben Millard
Marshall Fields' Commissionaire Agent 178
Mary (Francis) Hull 6
Massacre of Wounded Knee 160
Master Planning 124, 125

McCoy................................*See* Mr. John McCoy
meadowlarks..............................139, 140, 141
Melanoplus sanguinipes...............................55
memorial brochure 78
Michael Stricklin 130
Migratory Bird Treaty Act of 1918 75
mile track.......................51, *See* Ruskin Park Racetrack
Millard Ridge 3, 18, 89, 112, 140, 166
Millard Ridge Dedication, June 28th, 1957 ...*See* Ben Millard
Millard's donation 128
Millard-Keys-Haskell...................................26
Millard's donation 122
Milner Report 124, 172
Milwaukee Railroad Line 88
minerals.............................97, 98, 140, 178
Miniconjou 160
Minnesota3, 6, 11, 31, 42, 43, 63, 69, 77, 97, 109, 114, 140, 171, 180
Minnetonka Moccasins 128
Mission 66 ....173, 174
Mission 66 planning concepts 174
Missouri ....*See* Missouri River
Missouri River 6, 7, 8, 9, 10, 15, 75, 88, 171
Mitchell South Dakota Evening Republican............41
Mitchell, South Dakota................................88
monument headquarters 125
moonshine 62
Morin and Colten Wholesale Grocers............48
motion picture producer..............................49
motorcycle race 37
Mount Rushmore 71, 74, 84
movie camera, 16 mm 156
Mr. and Mrs. Walt Starr 51
My father ....*See* Glen Millard

N

national monument proposal 104
national park designation...........................82, 89
National Park Service90, 98, 100, 101, 102, 103, 111, 112, 119, 120, 121, 124, 164, 165, 169, 173
national park status 110
National Park System 76, 102
National Press Association 27
National Register.........................107, 174, 175
National Register of Historic Places 107
National Register under Criterion C 175
National Reserve Life Insurance 22, 57, 64, 78
National Scenic Byway 84
Native American help................................156
Native American spirit.................................66
Native American tea...................................141
Native American women.............................142
native fox ....*See* swift fox

native materials 125
Navajo and Zuni jewelry..........................117, 146
Navajo rugs and blankets 117
Needles Highway.............................72, 84, 85
Neno.......................*See* Stella Neely Millard
New Deal 104, 105, 114, 124
New Mexico 117, 179
New York 32, 60
Nick McNeely 182
ninth governor 72
Norbeck ....*See* US Senator Peter Norbeck
Norbeck's alter ego ....*See* Ben Millard
northern plains..67
Northwest Entrance Road 174
Norwegian 71
Nothing To Do Today 139
NPS...119, 120, 122, 123, 124, 127, 128, 136, 166, 172, 173
Nu Pi Sigma 115
NW Dirt Track Auto Association.....................40

O

Occidental College 114
Okinawa 117
Old Faithful Lodge 176
Old Settler's Picnic 33
Omaha & Northern Nebraska Railway 10
Oregon trail 170
original dining room 152
Ozzie Klavestad 157

P

pack rat 157, 178
pack rat den 150
Palmers Drug Store 90
Park Extension...102
park rangers 141
Park Service ....*See* National Park Service
Park Superintendent Howard StricklinSee Chief Ranger Howard R. Strickland
part of Henry Ferguson ....*See* Glen Millard
party line telephones 87
Patty Millard 2, 3, 139, 140, 154, 158
Peace Corps..4, 181
Pender, Nebraska..6
perfect pitch ....*See* Glen Millard
Peru 181
Peter N. Norbeck Holiday.............................74
Peter Norbeck..............*See* US Senator Peter Norbeck
Peter Norbeck Scenic Byway 84
petrified wood.............................97, 98, 140
pheasant hunting 31, 75
photography..163

Pierre, South Dakota 24
Pine Ridge Indian Reservation 8, 102, 156, 157, 160
Pinnacles.. 85, 86, 87, 90, 93, 94, 95, 96, 116, 117, 120, 122, 125, 127, 130, 131, 134
Pinnacles Checking Station 120
pioneer families 109
plains states 106
plainsman, George Millard..169
Playground of the Prairie 30, 38
poison gas 69, 119
Pollock v. Farmers Loan & Trust Co. 20
post office 12, 87
prairie chickens 132
prairie dog towns 165
prairie fires 9
prairie flowers 164
Prairie Home Companion 171
Prairie Homestead 107
Presentation College 75
preservation and conservation of the natural landscape 125
President Calvin Coolidge...75
president of the Black Hills National Bank*See* Robert E. Driscoll
President of the Institute......................*See* Dr. Evan Davies
presidential proclamation 110
preventive maintenance 127
Private Joseph Whitehouse...62
Professor Croan 13, 14
Progressive movement...................................4, 74, 76, 81
progressive Republican 5, 76
progressivism............................*See* Progressive movement
Prohibition 62
project manager..102
protection of local industry..19
Public Roads Administration 120

Q

Quinn...*See* Quinn, South Dakota
Quinn, South Dakota 86

R

R.E. Dowdell ....*See* Dowdell
racetrack 38
railroads 11, 54
Ranger Shuler ....*See* Jay Shuler
Rapid ....*See* Rapid City, South Dakota
Rapid City Commercial Club 83
Rapid City, South Dakota..12, 87
rationing..127, 137
REA (Rural Electrical Association) 65
Red Wing..69

Redfield, South Dakota 71
refreshment stand 90
regional drought...55, 58
reintroduced 164
reintroduced bill...88, 165
reservation 157, 158, 159
Resettlement Administration....................................105
Revenue Act of 1862 19
Revenue Act of 1913 21
revenue purposes 19
Rexford G. Tugwell 105
Richard Layne 41, 179
Richard Varco 31, 66, 180
Riley Millard family ....*See* Riley Milton Millard
Riley Milton Millard...6
Rilla and Albert Thompson 142, 145
Rise Studio ....*See* Chuck Orelup
riverboats 10
Roaring Twenties 38
Robert E. Dowdell...............................*See* Dowdell
Robert E. Driscoll 18
Robert E. Geiger 60
Robert Emmett Dowdell..........................*See* Dowdell
Robert Orelup 180
Rocky Montain big horn sheep 164
Rocky Mountain Locust...56
Rodee Ranch 34
Rodee's Grove 52
Rodney Sando 181
Roger Kennedy 170
Roman Catholicism 160
Roosevelt Republican..76
Roosevelt's first 100 days in office.............................104
Rosie the Riveter 137
Ruskin Park 2, 3, 4, 11, 15, 24, 25, 26, 27, 28, 30, 31, 32, 33, 34, 35, 36, 38, 39, 40, 41, 42, 43, 44, 45, 47, 48, 49, 50, 51, 52, 63, 66, 88, 91, 115, 116, 133, 179, 180
Ruskin Park Chautauqua Grounds.................................32
Ruskin Park Hunting Club 36
Ruskin Park Marker 30
Ruskin Park plays 25
Ruskin Park racetrack 30
Ruskin Park Stock Company 49
Ruth Norbeck 68, 69

S

Sage Creek Basin 103
Sage Hen 77
Sanborn County 24, 26, 30, 33, 34, 38, 52, 105
Sanborn County Advocate 24, 26, 34
Sanborn Weekly Journal 32, 33, 37, 43, 52
Sandhills Region 170
Santee 52

Scandinavian tour bus 167
Scenic, South Dakota 87
SD Public Radio .... See Joe Tlustos
Secretary of the Interior 90
Senator Norbeck .... See US Senator Peter Norbeck
Senator Nye 93
September 4,th 1926 .... See wedding
sewer system 128
Shakopee, Minnesota 157
sharp-tailed grouse 132, 158
Shawn 182
Sheep Mountain Area 103
Sheep Mountain Canyon road 120
Shenandoah Normal College 8, 13
Shenandoah, Iowa 13
Shields 61
Shuler .... See Jay Shuler
Sioux Falls, South Dakota 15, 17, 93, 181
Sioux Indian taco 142
Sitting Bull 160
Sixteenth Amendment 20
small gasoline tractors 59
small-town South Dakota banker .... See Ben Millard
Smithsonian Guide to Historic America
    The Plains States 169
sod house .... See Prairie Homestead
South America 178
South Dakota Department of Banking 67
South Dakota Highway Department 85, 90
South Dakota highway engineer 83
South Dakota Legislature .... See Dowdell
South Dakota Press Association 26
South Dakota Public Radio and TV 40
South Dakota Rock and Roll Hall of Fame 36
South Dakota State Banking Department 57
South Dakota State College 69
South Dakota State Department of Banking See South
    Dakota State Banking Department
South Dakota State Gem .... See Fairburn agates
South Dakota State Historic Preservation Office (SDSHPO)
    174
South Dakota State Historical Society Markers 30
South Dakota State Senate 24
South Dakota. State House of Representatives 24
Speedway at Ruskin Park .... See Ruskin Park Racetrack
spiced buffalo meat .... See Sioux Indian taco
Spink County 71, 75
Spotted Elk 160
Spring Exposition 48
St. Paul, Minnesota 11, 63, 93, 171
Stables 51
Standard Radiator Company 48
Standing Rock Indian Reservation 160
State Bank of Interior 79

State Carnival of Sports 37
State Fair World's Fair Band 33
State Game Lodge 75, 84
State Game Park Reserve 84
State Highway 44 87
state of South Dakota 71, 120
State Representative Julie Bartling 74
Stella .... See Stella Neely Millard
Stella Neely Millard 16, 18, 21, 25, 43, 69, 94, 95, 96, 114,
    117, 118, 121, 129, 130, 131, 132, 133, 134, 135, 136,
    139, 142, 143, 144, 145, 146, 147, 148, 150, 154, 155,
    156, 157, 161, 162, 163, 178, 179, 180
Stephan Glen 181
Stephen Mather 124
Steve .... See Stella Neely
Stewart Warner 135
stock market collapse 54
stock market crash 58
Submarginal Land Division of the National Park Service. 101
subsurface 175
Sunday World-Herald newspaper 168
Superintendent Frank A. Hjort 173
Superior National Forest 77
Supreme Court 20
swamp cooler 96
swift fox 165
Sylvan Lake 72
Syracuse, New York 45

T

Tariff Act, 1894 19
tax extension relief 20
Ted E. Hustead 100
ten-year program .... See Mission 66
tepee 141, 155
The Corps .... See Corps of Discovery
the pass .... 70, See Cedar Pass
Theinsens Opera House 46
Theodore Roosevelt 176
Theresa Fire Thunder 143
Thomas .... See Fred Thomas
Thomas Vint 124
Tom and Martha Boothroyd 142
Tom Barkdull 38
traveling motion picture studio 179
triple whammy 51
Tuesy Johnson 142
Two Grey Hills Trading Post 117

U

Uncle Herb .... See Herbert Millard
Uncle Herbert .... See Herbert Millard

University of Chicago 114, 115
University of Chicago Library 116
University of Minnesota..........................157
University of Nebraska 118
University of South Dakota 69
Uruguay..........................181
US Black Baseball League 37
US Civil War...........................6
US Congressional Record 3
US Department of Agriculture Entomologist 55
US entrance into World War II...........................136
US Highway 14 68
US National Park System 68
US Navy.........................96, 97, 117, 132, 138, 142
US officers school...........................114
US President Theodore Roosevelt...........................76
US Senator Peter Norbeck4, 39, 67, 68, 71, 72, 74, 75, 76, 77, 78, 79, 80, 81, 82, 83, 84, 85, 86, 88, 89, 90, 91, 92, 100, 101, 102, 103, 104, 110, 111, 113, 124, 167, 169, 171
US Senator Peter Norbeck's letters...........................67
US Senator Richard F Pettigrew 33
USS *New Mexico* (*BB-40*)...........................117
Utah 77

V

Vermillion, South Dakota 69, 71, 102
Vic. ....*See* Victor Walker
Vic Zimmerman 31
Vice President Walter F. Mondale 182
Victor ....*See* Victor Walker
Victor Walker 117, 145
Virginia Ravens...........................92

W

W. A. Loveland...........................12, 15, 24, 66
Wa-kar-me...........................*See* Chief Blackbird
Wall Drug Store 100
Walter and Dagmar Siegenthaler...........................30, 52
wandering cattle 123, 139
War Production Board 138
Washington, D.C...........................60, 91
wedding...........................68, 70, 79
Weekly State Spirit of Huron 44
West River country...........................94
Western Airlines...........................139
Western Normal College 13, 14, 15
white lightning 62
White River 72, 73, 78, 122, 131, 156, 167
White River Badlands 72, 78
Whittier High School 44, 114
Whittier, California...........................43, 116

Wild West...........................10, 160
Willard Sharp...........................159
William Clark 61
William Safire 104
Wind Cave National Park...........................72, 121
Wind River Range...........................170
Winter Headquarters. Los Angeles, Cal............49
Woman's Athletic Association 115
women's economic advantage 137
women's suffrage...........................76
Woonsocket News...........................46
Woonsocket, South Dakota...........................33
Works Progress Administration (WPA) 120, 136
World War I 19, 21, 37, 57, 62, 69
World War II 96, 113, 126, 137, 173
World War II whammy...........................137
Wounded Knee Massacre..*See* Massacre of Wounded Knee
Wyoming 165

Y

Yellow Mounds Area 86
Yellowstone National Park 176